CLOSER

EACH DAY

A 90-DAY DEVOTIONAL

TO GROW STEADY AND STRONG

ADRIAN ROGERS

Closer Each Day

Adrian Rogers

Published by Love Worth Finding Ministries, Inc.
                Memphis TN 38183-0300

Words in brackets within scripture quotations added for clarity. Unless otherwise marked, all scripture taken from the New King James Version. Copyright © 1982 by Thomas Nelson, Inc. Used by permission. All rights reserved.

f you've ever felt like you can't keep steady in your faith—that distractions pull you away, or that your best intentions don't always last—you're not alone. The good news is that God isn't asking you to prove your strength. He delights to show His strength in your weakness.

Walking with Jesus doesn't happen in giant leaps but in steady, daily steps. Every day offers a new opportunity to draw near to Him, to hear His voice through Scripture, and to let His truth shape your life. This devotional was created to help you take those daily steps, growing closer each day to the Savior who loves you.

Each reading follows a simple rhythm rooted in the way Pastor Adrian Rogers often encouraged believers to approach God's Word: pray, ponder, and practice. You'll begin by praying over a passage of Scripture, asking God to open your heart to His truth. Then you'll ponder a devotional thought from Pastor Rogers' preaching—timeless truth made simple. Finally, you'll find a reflection question or a practical step to put God's Word into action.

Over the next 90 days, may you discover that steadiness doesn't come from your own strength but from God's faithful presence as you walk with Him, one step at a time.

1

PRAY OVER THIS

Then Jesus said to those Jews who believed Him, "If you
abide in My word, you are My disciples indeed. And you shall
know the truth, and the truth shall make you free."

JOHN 8:31-32

PONDER THIS When you believe in Jesus and you continue in the Word, you know the truth, and you become liberated. Many today believe in the Lord Jesus Christ and are going to Heaven. But you are not a liberated person because you have never really absorbed the truth. You have never taken to the truth; you've never taken time to buy the truth. Do you know the word in that sentence that is key? *Disciple*. Do you know another word akin to disciple? *Discipline*. People don't like discipline because they want to be free. They see truth and discipline as restrictive.

I read a quote somewhere. I don't know who said it, but it stuck in my heart. "He who is a slave to the compass is the master of the oceans; the rest have to sail close to the shore." The compass is what the ancient mariners used to guide their ships. That restriction gives them freedom and mastery of so much more than they could decipher on their own. Truth liberates you. Truth makes you free.

- What are some guiding principles you want to take into this new year?

- What is the difference between hearing the truth and absorbing the truth?

PRACTICE THIS Spend time writing down some verses from God's Word and consider how these truths apply to your life.

（2）

Buy the truth, and do not sell it, also wisdom
and instruction and understanding.
PROVERBS 23:23

PONDER THIS As a Bible student, you need to measure and test everything you read by the Word of God. You have a grid that everything must pass through. You have a radar. All truth intersects, and one of the tests of any good book is this: When you put that book down, do you begin to think? All genuine truth intersects because all real truth is of God. God did not make you to be a reservoir of facts— He meant for you to be a channel of truth. If you're growing in knowledge but not growing in grace, you're going to be dangerous. I've met those people. They can split a theological hair into nine separate sections, but they're not growing in the grace of our Lord and Savior Jesus Christ.

Some people just want to study methods. You will never get excited about methods unless you learn the truth behind the method. Why do you do this? Are you experiencing freedom? Real truth, as Jesus says, sets you free. In your study, ask yourself these questions: *Am I learning humility? Am I sharing grace with others in the process? Am I being set free?*

- What is the difference between living as a reservoir of facts and as a channel of truth?

- What truth have you learned recently? How has it impacted you?

PRACTICE THIS Speak with a friend in Christ about what you have been learning and discuss how it has affected you.

3

PRAY OVER THIS

For the word of God is living and powerful, and sharper
than any two-edged sword, piercing even to the division
of soul and spirit, and of joints and marrow, and is a
discerner of the thoughts and intents of the heart.

HEBREWS 4:12

PONDER THIS The Word of God is such a sharp instrument that if it were a literal sword, it could divide joints and marrow. Since it's a spiritual sword, it divides the soul and the spirit. Do you know the difference between the soul and the spirit? I was preaching for a long time, and I didn't know the difference between the soul and the spirit. I just thought that was the invisible part of a human being. You could call it his soul, you could call it his spirit—six of one, half a dozen of another. But the more I studied, the more I found out that the spirit is what makes man absolutely unique and in the image of God.

Plants have bodies, but they don't have souls. Animals have bodies and souls, but they don't have a spirit. Only Man has a spirit because Man is made in the image of God and God is spirit. "Those who worship Him must worship Him in spirit and truth" (John 4:24). How important it is, then, that we have an instrument that can divide between soul and spirit.

So much of the trouble we get into in the spiritual world is because we cannot divide between soul and spirit. The reason we don't divide between soul and spirit is that we do not know the Word of God as we should.

- How have you been guided by God's truth in the past? How is it guiding you today?

- Why do you think we struggle to use the powerful tool of Scripture in our lives?

PRACTICE THIS Write down a verse to memorize this week.

PRAY OVER THIS

For I am not ashamed of the gospel of Christ, for it is the power of
God to salvation for everyone who believes, for the Jew first and
also for the Greek. For in it the righteousness of God is revealed
from faith to faith; as it is written, "The just shall live by faith."

ROMANS 1:16-17

PONDER THIS There was a Roman Catholic monk named Martin Luther. He wanted to be right with God, and he was doing all he could. He'd tried. He'd worked. He'd fasted. He'd prayed. He took a pilgrimage to Rome, and there he found what is called the Santa Scala—the Holy Stairs. These were reported to have been the stairs Jesus Christ had climbed in Pilate's judgment hall. People thought that if they could get on their knees on those stairs and say their prayers while climbing those stairs, then maybe they could be forgiven for their sins. So, Martin Luther was there on his knees, one step at a time, praying, "Oh God, oh God, I want to know You. I want to be right with You." But when he got to the top of those stairs, he was not any closer to God than he had been. But he had been studying the Book of Romans, and there a light burst into his heart and into his mind.

Romans 1:17b says, "The just shall live by faith." And he realized, "I'm not saved by my good works. I'm not saved by my religion. I'm not saved by my ritual. I'm not saved by my good intentions. I am saved by the grace of God when I put my faith in what Jesus did for me on the cross." Martin Luther was born again, and the Protestant Reformation, which changed the entire world, began in 1517.

- Have you ever tried to do something to get closer to God? Why will our own works never help us be right with God?

- Why do we at times believe the lie that works will save us? How has following Jesus changed your perspective on your works?

PRACTICE THIS Share with others how following Jesus has changed your life.

5

Paul, a bondservant of Jesus Christ, called to be an
apostle, separated to the gospel of God.
ROMANS 1:1

PONDER THIS Not only was Paul a saved man, but he was also a surrendered man. Notice what he called himself: "Paul, a bondservant." The word *servant* is the Greek word *doulos*, and it literally means "slave." Paul said, "I'm a slave of Jesus."

You may say, "I don't want to be a slave." But you already are. Everybody is a slave to something or someone. If you're in bondage to sin, you're in the worst kind of slavery. The unsaved man says, "I won't be free." As he seeks freedom, he goes into the worst bondage of all, the bondage of sin. But when a person comes to the Lord Jesus and says, "You are Lord. You are Master," he or she receives glorious freedom. John 8:36 says, "Therefore if the Son makes you free, you shall be free indeed."

What is the freedom of being a slave to the Lord Jesus Christ? It doesn't mean His will instead of my will; it means His will *is now* my will. When you understand this, many things will come to light in your heart and mind. May we come to God and say, "Lord, I yield my will to You."

- When have you struggled with God and been a slave to sin?

- What does it look like to have God's will as your will?

PRACTICE THIS Talk to a Christian you look up to and ask how his or her will has changed to be God's will.

PRAY OVER THIS

Paul, a bondservant of Jesus Christ, called to be an
apostle, separated to the gospel of God.
ROMANS 1:1

PONDER THIS Paul was separated to the Gospel of God. Christians are to be separated. Christians are to be different. We are to stand out. Now, the kind of separation Paul had already been practicing was the separation of a Pharisee. The very word *Pharisee* implies separation. Paul was separated. Some people say, "Well, I live a separated Christian life. I don't smoke; I don't chew; and I don't go with the girls who do. I am separated." Well, a fence post doesn't smoke or chew or go with girls who do. So, you don't have any more religion than a fence post if that's what your separation is. And quitting those things will not make you more like the Lord Jesus Christ. You can walk the straight and narrow, and say, "I don't do this. I don't do this. I don't do this," and you'll be a proud, bitter Pharisee. That's what Paul was before he met the Lord Jesus Christ. He was already a Pharisee. He was already separated *from*, but he became separated *to*, and that is the difference.

The word *separated* here is the word in Greek from which we get our word *horizon*. Have you ever been up on a tall building and looked as far as you could see until the earth dips over? That is the horizon. And your horizon changes when your center changes. And when Jesus Christ is the center of your life, then your entire horizon has changed.

- What has changed since Jesus became the center of your life?

- What is the difference between being separated from the world and being separated to Jesus?

PRACTICE THIS Share with someone the testimony about how Jesus changed your horizon and perspective on life.

PRAY OVER THIS

...which He promised before through His prophets in the Holy Scriptures, concerning His Son Jesus Christ our Lord, who was born of the seed of David according to the flesh, and declared to be the Son of God with power according to the Spirit of holiness, by the resurrection from the dead. Through Him we have received grace and apostleship for obedience to the faith among all nations for His name, among whom you also are the called of Jesus Christ.

ROMANS 1:2-6

PONDER THIS The Gospel of God that Paul was dedicated to is not a so-called gospel that merely mentions Jesus or that only alludes to Jesus: Jesus is the Gospel.

Do you know why we have churches filled with moral worldlings? They have religion, but they've never met Jesus Christ. Christianity is not a creed, not a code, not a cause; it is Christ. But you cannot take Jesus Christ out of Christianity and still have Christianity. It's like taking the water out of a well, notes out of music, numbers out of mathematics. So many people have had an encounter with religion. But religion is not the Gospel. The source of the Gospel is God. The subject of the Gospel is Jesus. The supply of the Gospel is grace. Poor, lost, ruined sinners like we are saved by the glorious Gospel of our Lord and Savior Jesus Christ.

- When have you mistaken the Gospel for something other than Jesus?

- How can you tell when you are more focused on religion than you are on Jesus?

PRACTICE THIS Write down some areas in which you struggle to extend grace to others. Lift these burdens up to God, asking Him to help you stay fixed on Jesus, the subject of the Gospel.

PRAY OVER THIS

I am a debtor both to Greeks and to barbarians, both to
wise and to unwise. So, as much as is in me, I am ready to
preach the gospel to you who are in Rome also.

ROMANS 1:14-15

PONDER THIS Suppose there is a man in this state sentenced to be executed for a capital crime. Suppose the governor of this state calls you and says, "I'm going to pardon that man." And the governor tells you, "I want you to take this pardon to the prison and deliver it to the warden of the prison." So, you take that pardon, put it in your pocket, and then remember your wife told you to pick up a gallon of milk on the way home, so you do that. Sometime later, you're having your coffee and reading the newspaper, and some print jumps out at you. The man who was pardoned has just been executed! You happen to be wearing the same coat, and you pull out the pardon. He had been pardoned, but you had never delivered the message. How would you feel? How will you feel when the clouds fall on the casket of your next-door neighbor, and you never ever even told him about Jesus Christ? What about your mother, your brother, your father, your sister? Paul said, "I am a debtor. I've been saved by the grace of God. Jesus paid it all...but all to Him I owe." Do you know what this world needs? It needs followers of Jesus who have compassion for lost people. We're blessed, but we are an island of blessing surrounded by an ocean of need.

- Who in your life shares the Gospel with urgency?

- What are some things that distract you from the spiritual needs of those around you?

PRACTICE THIS Make a list of the spiritual needs around you and pray for them.

9

For I am not ashamed of the gospel of Christ, for it is the power of God to salvation for everyone who believes, for the Jew first and also for the Greek.

ROMANS 1:16

PONDER THIS Of the billions of people who've ever lived, only a handful have made a true mark on history. I'm talking about scientists, philosophers, rulers, military people, only a handful. But there's one name that stands above all other names, and that is the name of Jesus. Right now, there are multiplied millions of people attending to His Words and seeking to do His will. That one name that is above every name. Are you ashamed of Jesus Christ?

A young preacher had been called out of a life of sin to preach the Gospel of Jesus Christ. He thoroughly repented of his sin and was made new. But somebody who knew his old life wrote him a note and said, "Aren't you ashamed of yourself? You're up there telling people to get right with God." That person had known this man in his past and listed all his sins in detail. Do you know what the young preacher did? He read that note, bowed his head in prayer, stood up, and said, "Ladies and gentlemen, I've received a note, and here's what it says." Then, in front of that whole crowd, he read every one of those sins without leaving out one. And then he said this, "Yes, I am ashamed of myself, but I am not ashamed of my Savior." I hope I'll never be ashamed of Him.

- What are some parts of your testimony you have been ashamed of?

- When have you seen someone live unashamed of the Gospel? How did that impact you?

PRACTICE THIS Make a list of what it looks like to live unashamed of the Gospel. What attributes of living unashamed do you exhibit? Are there changes you need to make?

10

PRAY OVER THIS

For since the creation of the world His invisible attributes are clearly
seen, being understood by the things that are made, even His eternal
power and Godhead, so that they are without excuse, because, although
they knew God, they did not glorify Him as God, nor were thankful, but
became futile in their thoughts, and their foolish hearts were darkened.

ROMANS 1:20-21

PONDER THIS God has two witnesses that say He exists—creation and
conscience. The inner is the subjective witness of conscience; the outer is the
objective witness of creation. The blazing stars and this Universe—how did
it happen? To be an atheist, you have to believe that nothing times nobody
equals everything. But God has set His witness in the sky. Psalm 19:1-4 says, "The
heavens declare the glory of God; and the firmament shows His handiwork. Day
unto day utters speech, and night unto night reveals knowledge. There is no
speech nor language where their voice is not heard. Their line has gone out
through all the earth, and their words to the end of the world. In them He has
set a tabernacle for the sun." Anybody, any place, any time can go out and look
up at the stars and conclude, "That didn't just happen."

In the French Revolution, a revolutionary told a French peasant as they were
pulling down the churches and destroying the houses of worship, "Peasant, we're
going to destroy everything that reminds you of God." And the peasant pointed
to the stars and said, "Begin with those stars." The heavens declare the glory of
God.

- What parts of creation remind you of God's handiwork?

- How do you respond when you are reminded of who God is?

PRACTICE THIS Sit in creation or look out the window and praise God for who He
is according to His handiwork.

PRAY OVER THIS

For the wrath of God is revealed from heaven against all
ungodliness and unrighteousness of men, who suppress the
truth in unrighteousness, because what may be known of
God is manifest in them, for God has shown it to them.

ROMANS 1:18-19

PONDER THIS Suppose I were to pluck some parts out of nowhere, just cause them to appear, and then put them in a bucket and shake them around for a while, and then they become a button and then after a while a compass; and then after a while a steam gauge; and then after a while a speedometer, and then a gas meter, and finally a watch. I'm wearing the watch, and I tell you, "That's the way it came about." You'd say, "Adrian, I just don't believe that." Of course not! How could such a thing happen? But somehow, people have thought that something as wonderful as the human eye just simply happened.

Now I looked up the word *suppress*, in many translations, and let me give you some of them. Other translations include "hold back the truth," "smother the truth," "repress the truth," and "stifle the truth." All of them mean essentially the same thing—they resist and seek to hold back the truth of God. They do not want to know. Now, blindness is tragic, but willful blindness is horrible. There are none so blind as those who put out their own eyes. It's not that they cannot believe; it is that they will not believe.

- How do you regularly recognize God as the maker of all things?

- When are you tempted to ignore or suppress the truth found in Scripture?

PRACTICE THIS Talk with a fellow believer about any areas in which you need to hold to the truth and ask your friend to help hold you accountable.

PRAY OVER THIS

Do you not know that you are the temple of God and that the Spirit of God dwells in you? If anyone defiles the temple of God, God will destroy him. For the temple of God is holy, which temple you are.

1 CORINTHIANS 3:16-17

PONDER THIS As the body of Christ, we're in it together. What affects you affects me. And you cannot say, "What I do is nobody else's business." Not in the covenant relationship of a church. When one member suffers, every member suffers; when a part of my body is sick, the rest of my body feels it. I cannot isolate any member of my body and say, "Well, that doesn't really make any difference to me." The Church is the body of the Lord Jesus Christ, and I beg you, please, if there's immorality in your heart and your life, get right or get out! Don't hurt the body of Christ. Don't sing in the choir. Don't play in the orchestra. Don't sit on the platform. Don't preach from the pulpit if you are willfully ignoring sin.

You say, "Pastor, are you telling me that I can't come here for help if I have a problem?" Yes, that's what we're for. We are a society of sinners who finally realized it and have banded ourselves together to do something about it. Church is the only organization I know of in which you have to profess to be bad before you can join. But what I'm saying is this: if you think that your sin is a minor sin, something you intend to practice. If you've not come for help and encouragement, and if you do not have a repentant spirit, then you're in the wrong place. You have sinned against the Church, and the Bible says, "If anyone defiles the temple of God, God will destroy him," because you've defiled something that is pure and holy.

- What are some sinful habits you have let slide in your life?
- What would it look like to take our sins seriously in the Church?

PRACTICE THIS Pray and confess your sin to God. Repent and turn away from sin through the power of the Holy Spirit.

13

PRAY OVER THIS

The fool has said in his heart, "There is no God." They are corrupt, they have done abominable works, there is none who does good. The LORD looks down from heaven upon the children of men, to see if there are any who understand, who seek God. They have all turned aside, they have together become corrupt; there is none who does good, no, not one. Have all the workers of iniquity no knowledge, who eat up my people as they eat bread, and do not call on the LORD? There they are in great fear, for God is with the generation of the righteous. You shame the counsel of the poor, but the LORD is his refuge.

PSALM 14:1-6

PONDER THIS Years back, there was a young man, an atheist, at one of the local universities, who wrote about how the world would be better without Christians. He was very arrogant, but he came to a church where I was ministering in Florida. He really came to show off, to argue, and to make fun. But the finger of God touched him, he came under conviction, and he got saved. I called him into my office. I wanted to talk to him because I wanted to know what happened in his life and how a man like him could be so poisoned against the things of God. And so, I talked to him about his faith. Then I said to him, "George, tell me why you were an atheist." He said, "Mr. Rogers, before I came to this church, before I heard the Gospel, and before I gave my heart to Jesus Christ, I was so sure there is no God." He said, "And now, I can't even remember the arguments." The problem was not in his head; it was in his heart. It wasn't that he *could* not believe, it was that he *would* not believe. There is a willful self-determination when people hold back and suppress the truth.

- What are some of the things of God that are hard for you to believe?

- Why do we struggle to let the truth of God penetrate our hearts?

PRACTICE THIS Lift up in prayer the truth of God from His Word and allow it to penetrate your heart.

PRAY OVER THIS

You shall have no other gods before Me. You shall not make
for yourself a carved image—any likeness of anything that is in
heaven above, or that is in the earth beneath, or that is in the
water under the earth; you shall not bow down to them nor
serve them. For I, the LORD your God, am a jealous God, visiting
the iniquity of the fathers upon the children to the third and
fourth generations of those who hate Me, but showing mercy to
thousands, to those who love Me and keep My commandments."

EXODUS 20:3-6

PONDER THIS Do you know what an idol is? An idol is a magnified sinner. People take their worst vices of war, greed, lust, and pride, and make gods out of them. People make gods out of their vices, then they worship their vices by participating in them. The sinner molds the idol, and then the idol molds the sinner.

You may say, "But, Adrian, this is the United States of America, and we don't have idols here." Who are you kidding? What is an idol? An idol is anything a person loves more, fears more, serves more, or values more than God. For example, the Bible says people are "lovers of pleasures rather than lovers of God," in 2 Timothy 3:4. We exchange the glory of Almighty God for these kinds of things. And we've learned the way of the heathen through idolatry.

- Why is it important to take idols seriously?

- What are some things that can be idols that are not carved images?

PRACTICE THIS Consider what may be an idol in your life according to the definition, "anything you love, fear, serve, or value more than God."

PRAY OVER THIS

"Come now, and let us reason together," says the LORD, "Though your sins are like scarlet, they shall be as white as snow; though they are red like crimson, they shall be as wool. If you are willing and obedient, you shall eat the good of the land; but if you refuse and rebel, you shall be devoured by the sword"; for the mouth of the LORD has spoken.

ISAIAH 1:18-20

PONDER THIS You may say, "Pastor, you made me feel bad with this message about sin, because, very frankly, my life has been touched by immorality." I want to tell you something, that's what this Book is all about—good news! It's the bad news that makes the good news good. The Bible says of the Gospel of the Lord Jesus Christ, "it is the power of God to salvation" (Romans 1:16b). God is a God of grace; God is a God of forgiveness; God is a God of another chance; and God is a God who says, "Though your sins are like scarlet they shall be as white as snow; though they are red like crimson, they shall be as wool." Hallelujah for such a Gospel. Thank God for this: "Therefore, if anyone is in Christ, he is a new creation; old things have passed away; behold, all things have become new" (2 Corinthians 5:17).

There's one thing God will never accept when it comes to sin, and that is an excuse. But when there comes a confession, thank God. The cleansing tides of Calvary sweep across the human soul, and every blot, blur, and blemish is washed whiter than snow by Jesus' blood.

- When have you been overwhelmed with guilt? How did the Gospel impact you at that time?

- Why do you think we feel tempted to give excuses and alibis instead of confessing our sin to God?

PRACTICE THIS Share with a friend how the Gospel has impacted the way you experience sin, confession, and forgiveness.

PRAY OVER THIS

Therefore you are inexcusable, O man, whoever you are who judge, for in whatever you judge another you condemn yourself; for you who judge practice the same things. But we know that the judgment of God is according to truth against those who practice such things. And do you think this, O man, you who judge those practicing such things, and doing the same, that you will escape the judgment of God?

ROMANS 2:1-3

PONDER THIS It's time we stop thinking primarily about others and begin to think about and examine ourselves. Even we who are saved may be guilty of hypocrisy. It is foolish to say, "Faults in others I can see, but praise the Lord, there are none in me." We tend to want to measure ourselves by other people. We want to play the comparison game. The problem is that God measures us by the perfect standard: Himself.

The word *hypocrite* means "play actor." In past times, the actors would put on disguises. If they were supposed to be happy, rather than merely acting happy, they would put on a happy face, a disguise. If they were to be sad, they'd put on a sad face. If they were to be fierce, they'd put on a fierce face. They wore masks. And Jesus essentially said, "In the religious world, there are some who are hypocrites—they are actors who are wearing disguises." But Paul said in the passage above, "the judgment of God is according to truth." God is going to pull off the mask; there will be no disguise. The standard will not be profession, pretension, or performance. Truth is the standard.

- Why is it important to confess our hypocrisy to God?

- What are some areas in which you see hypocrisy in your life?

PRACTICE THIS Spend time in the Word, asking God to show you areas of hypocrisy in your life. Be ready to confess and repent in these areas.

PRAY OVER THIS

Or do you despise the riches of His goodness, forbearance, and
longsuffering, not knowing that the goodness of God leads you to
repentance? But in accordance with your hardness and your impenitent
heart you are treasuring up for yourself wrath in the day of wrath
and revelation of the righteous judgment of God, who "will render to
each one according to his deeds": eternal life to those who by patient
continuance in doing good seek for glory, honor, and immortality.

ROMANS 2:4-7

PONDER THIS Some people have the idea that if they're not having any problems, they're right with God. If they're healthy, if their bank account is up, if they have no problems, evidently God loves them, and everything is fine. They don't need to repent—look at all those blessings. But the blessings of God don't mean you're right with God. God gives you blessings to bring you to Him. It doesn't mean you don't need repentance. The goodness of God leads to repentance.

As a matter of fact, the goodness of God only makes your judgment more severe if you deny your dependence on Him. If you're being blessed now, let me beg you to come to the Lord Jesus Christ. Don't get the idea that God's goodness is an invitation to sin more, because the greater the blessings, the greater the judgment. And I want to remind you that Sodom and Gomorrah were at an all-time high when the fire and brimstone fell. The Bible says one of the marks of Sodom was that the people not only committed abominations but also had fullness of bread and idleness. (See Ezekiel 16:49-50.) In other words, there was so much prosperity that people didn't even have to work. But the goodness of God did not lead them to repentance.

- What is your typical posture before God when you are going through good times?

- Where do you consider yourself to be right now—in an easier or harder season? How can you practice repentance regardless of the season you are in?

PRACTICE THIS Speak with a friend about how your relationship with God changes when you are in a good or hard season.

PRAY OVER THIS

What then? Are we better than they? Not at all. For we have previously charged both Jews and Greeks that they are all under sin. As it is written: "There is none righteous, no, not one; there is none who understands; there is none who seeks after God."

ROMANS 3:9-11

PONDER THIS Sometimes we think that because of our environment or pedigree, we're excused or better. I preached one time at a church, and a lady could hardly wait to get to see me because my last name is Rogers. She said, "You, sir, are a Rogers." And she said, "I am a Rogers. My father was a Rogers, and my maiden name was Rogers." Then she just smiled and threw her shoulders back, and she said, "You know, I have studied our family background, and you will be pleased to know that we came over on the Mayflower." I said, "Well, that's interesting." I said, "I traced it back further than that." She said, "You did?" I said, "Yes, we have come all the way from a crooked farmer and a drunken sailor. The farmer was Adam, and the sailor was Noah, and we go all the way back." We are sinners by birth, by nature, by heritage. It doesn't matter about our race or our background.

The people in the Book of Romans wanted to stretch themselves out in the gutter alongside somebody else and say, "I'm better than he or she is." But you see, that's not the standard. The standard is the glory of God, and that's the reason Paul would say later in Romans 3:23, "For all have sinned and fall short of the glory of God." We need to quit comparing ourselves to one another.

- Why do we often struggle with comparison?
- To whom do you compare yourself? In what areas do you tend to compare yourself with others?

PRACTICE THIS Write down some areas of comparison you struggle with and bring them before God in prayer.

PRAY OVER THIS

But now the righteousness of God apart from the law is revealed, being witnessed by the Law and the Prophets, even the righteousness of God, through faith in Jesus Christ, to all and on all who believe. For there is no difference; for all have sinned and fall short of the glory of God, being justified freely by His grace through the redemption that is in Christ Jesus, whom God set forth as a propitiation by His blood, through faith, to demonstrate His righteousness, because in His forbearance God had passed over the sins that were previously committed, to demonstrate at the present time His righteousness, that He might be just and the justifier of the one who has faith in Jesus.

ROMANS 3:21-26

PONDER THIS The law cannot save you. God has given His holy law, but the law is given to show us we're sinners. What is the wisest thing you could do today? Shut up and plead guilty. That's what Paul is saying. This phrase has been used a lot in the wrong sense, but here's what he's saying: "That every mouth may be stopped" (Romans 3:19b). Essentially, God said, "Shut your mouth!" Then Scripture says, "That all the world may become guilty before God."

We won't know the mercy and forgiveness of the King until we admit our sin. So many times, we want to strut to Heaven. But here is the verdict of the court: All have sinned. God says, "Be quiet." Paul says, "Be quiet, every mouth, shut up, plead guilty." All have sinned, but thankfully, all can receive grace.

- Why do we struggle to plead guilty before God?
- When did you admit your guilt before God? How did that change your relationship with Him?

PRACTICE THIS Consider anything you may be thinking or doing that does not meet God's standard. Plead guilty before God; repent and receive His forgiveness.

PRAY OVER THIS

Therefore, just as the church is subject to Christ, so let the wives be to their own husbands in everything. Husbands, love your wives, just as Christ also loved the church and gave Himself for her, that He might sanctify and cleanse her with the washing of water by the word.

EPHESIANS 5:24-26

PONDER THIS You need to make a decision. Give your heart to Almighty God because He is the only One who can guide you. After you make that decision, depend on Him, and look to Him. He will deliver you from sexual immorality if you trust Him. After decision and dependence, you need devotion. Love God with all of your heart and love your own wife, your own husband, with a supernatural love. When the Bible says, "Husbands, love your wives," (Ephesians 5:25a) that's not a suggestion, that's not a request—it is a command, and anything God commands you to do, you can do.

Finally, you need development. Feed your love and help it to grow. Love is not like a diamond—something you find hard, brittle, and beautiful, and you keep it to save it. Love is like a flower; it's got to be cultivated, watered, cared for, and nurtured. If you don't love your wife more today than you did when you married her, you probably love her less. Continue to feed that love from day to day. Develop that love for God and for your spouse.

- In which area do you struggle the most: decision, dependence, devotion, or development?

- How has God's love helped you love others better?

PRACTICE THIS Love your spouse in an intentional way today. If you are not married, encourage a godly couple you appreciate.

PRAY OVER THIS

My heart is steadfast, O God, my heart is steadfast; I will sing
and give praise. Awake, my glory! Awake, lute and harp! I will
awaken the dawn. I will praise You, O LORD, among the peoples;
I will sing to You among the nations. For Your mercy reaches
unto the heavens, and Your truth unto the clouds. Be exalted, O
God, above the heavens; let Your glory be above all the earth.

PSALM 57:7-11

PONDER THIS Watch what you read and what you see. Decide there are certain things you are not going to watch. Discipline your life. You wouldn't put garbage in your mouth, so don't put garbage in your mind. And guard your company, too: "the companion of fools will be destroyed" (Proverbs 13:20b).

You also need to have determination to stay in the Lord's way. You also need to have determination to stay in the Lord's way. Joshua made it clear that, regardless of what others chose, he and his household would serve the Lord. (See Joshua 24:15.) And I love what the Psalmist said: "My heart is steadfast, O God." If you make up your mind about one big decision, you won't have to keep making up your mind about a lot of little decisions. Because your heart is fixed, you have determined, "Oh God, my God, I will serve You."

- What does it look like to be determined to live for the Lord?

- What are some ways you need to guard your company or your mind this week?

PRACTICE THIS Confess some of the ways you have failed to guard your mind. Ask God to lead you in His way to keep you steadfast.

PRAY OVER THIS

For what does the Scripture say? "Abraham believed God, and it was accounted to him for righteousness." Now to him who works, the wages are not counted as grace but as debt.

ROMANS 4:3-4

PONDER THIS Grace is the unmerited favor and kindness of God shown to one who does not deserve it and can never earn it. You will be saved by grace, or you won't be saved at all.

Sometimes when I speak, people introduce me and say nice things about me. But suppose someone said, "There's one thing about Adrian—you just can't believe him." No matter how many nice things you might say about me, if you say, "You can't believe him," you've just cut off the root of my character. The greatest thing you can do to glorify God is to believe God. Faith pleases God because it glorifies God, and because faith pleases God, God rewards faith.

What is faith? Faith is not saying, "God prove it to me, and then I'll believe it." No, faith is a response to the nature and character of God. Faith believes God, not for what God has done, but for who God is. When my eye is right, my eye responds to light. When my ear is right, my ear responds to sound. When my heart is right, my heart responds to God. That response is faith, and that faith glorifies God. If a man could be saved by works, God would not get the glory. But when a man is justified by faith, God gets the glory.

- When do you struggle most to believe God?

- When have you been happy that you believed God? What happened when you trusted Him?

PRACTICE THIS Take a step of faith and believe God in an area in which you have been struggling.

PRAY OVER THIS

For all have sinned and fall short of the glory of God, being justified freely by His grace through the redemption that is in Christ Jesus.

ROMANS 3:23-24

PONDER THIS When you are saved, sin will never be on your account again. God will not impute sin to you. Now you say, "Well, Pastor Rogers, what if I get saved and then I sin again?" Did I hear you say, "What if"? You know, some people have the idea that, "If I'm living right when I die, I'll go to Heaven." Do you think your goodness is going to get you to Heaven? No! "Blessed is he whose transgression is forgiven, whose sin is covered. Blessed is the man to whom the LORD does not impute iniquity, and in whose spirit there is no deceit" (Psalm 32:1-2). If He were to put one-half of one sin on your account, you'd die and go to Hell. God is a holy God, but He will not impute iniquity. Now that doesn't mean you can sin and get by with it. Sin is serious to God, and He deals with it seriously.

We need to keep a short account with God, confessing and repenting of our sins regularly. His grace is abundant, but it has come at a cost. It is a gift to be treasured, not squandered. He will not impute sin onto your account any longer. What amazing grace! When you understand grace, you can understand why John Newton wrote the famous line, "Amazing grace! How sweet the sound that saved a wretch like me."

- Where do you struggle to believe God will not count sin against you if you are in Christ?

- What makes God's grace seem too good to be true?

PRACTICE THIS Have a conversation with a friend about God's grace. Share the areas where it's hard for you to believe, seeking to encourage one another in the reality of God's grace.

(24)

PRAY OVER THIS

So Jesus said to them, "Because of your unbelief; for
assuredly, I say to you, if you have faith as a mustard seed,
you will say to this mountain, 'Move from here to there,' and
it will move; and nothing will be impossible for you."

MATTHEW 17:20

PONDER THIS Why is faith so important? The Bible says, "But without faith it is impossible to please Him" (Hebrews 11:6a). If you please God, it doesn't matter whom you displease. And if you displease God, it really doesn't matter whom you please. You can't be saved apart from faith. But anyone who is lost can be saved if he or she will put his or her faith where God put his or her sins—on the Lord Jesus Christ.

Faith not only saves us but also enables us to live the Christian life. Some Christians are stumbling and failing, while others are victorious. What is the difference? The difference is faith. Some Christians have a bright hope for Heaven. To others, it's not real. But for those who have faith, "Faith is the substance of things hoped for, the evidence of things not seen" (Hebrews 11:1). Faith makes a difference because it gives hope that goes beyond this life and present circumstances, no matter what.

- How would you assess your faith? How would you like to grow in your faith?

- Who is an example of someone you know with a strong faith? How have you seen that exemplified?

PRACTICE THIS Talk to a person whose faith you admire and ask how that strong faith was developed.

PRAY OVER THIS

Therefore, having been justified by faith, we have peace with God through our Lord Jesus Christ, through whom also we have access by faith into this grace in which we stand, and rejoice in hope of the glory of God. And not only that, but we also glory in tribulations, knowing that tribulation produces perseverance; and perseverance, character; and character, hope. Now hope does not disappoint, because the love of God has been poured out in our hearts by the Holy Spirit who was given to us.

ROMANS 5:1-5

PONDER THIS What is patience? Not the ability to thread a needle. Not the ability to finish a crossword puzzle. No, the word *patience* means "endurance." When the crisis comes, it doesn't make you; it reveals what you're made of. How many people would say, "Pastor, I want strength. I want victory. I want prosperity. I want contentment." We know just about everybody wants those things. But if I were to ask how many of you want patience, how many would speak up? However, you'll never have these other things without patience, steadfastness, and endurance. Tribulation works patience.

You will never learn much of anything of worth if you don't have endurance and patience. If you want to learn how to play the piano, you're going to have to learn the scales. If you're going to learn Greek, you're going to have to study the verbs. If you want to build character, you're going to have to persevere; you're going to have to endure. There is no instant maturity. Conversion brings conflict, and conflict is meant to teach continuance and constancy. The Bible calls it patience.

- Why is patience so difficult for us? How does God grow us in patience?

- When have you had to practice patience in your walk with the Lord? What have you learned from this?

PRACTICE THIS Pray and ask God to grow patience and endurance in you.

26

PRAY OVER THIS

"This hope we have as an anchor of the soul, both sure and
steadfast, and which enters the Presence behind the veil, where
the forerunner has entered for us, even Jesus, having become
High Priest forever according to the order of Melchizedek."

HEBREWS 6:19-20

PONDER THIS I heard a story about a family whose son grew critically ill, and he was dying at home. The conversation between the little boy and his father went something like this: The boy asked his dad, "Dad, am I going to die?" The father said, "Son, someday you will die. But don't worry about it. After you die, it will be all over. You won't feel anything; you won't know anything; you will have forgotten the pain and the sorrow. I love you, son. Just hold on, son. Then after a while, it'll be over." The son said, "But father, I'm afraid, and I don't want to die. I need some help." And the father said, "Son, I love you. Just hold on." The boy responded, "Father, you're telling me to hold on, but there's nothing to hold onto."

When you know Jesus and those chilly waters of death touch you and the winds are blowing, your anchor will hold. You will have a rock-solid faith. That's what hope means. Conversion brings conflict; conflict teaches constancy; constancy builds character; and character enables us to trust God in the darkest storm. Aren't you glad there is a certain hope?

- in your life does not have the anchor of the hope of the Gospel?

- How has this anchor changed how you handle the crises and worries of life?

PRACTICE THIS Write down some verses that remind you there is a secure hope in God.

27

PRAY OVER THIS

Who, contrary to hope, in hope believed, so that he became
the father of many nations, according to what was spoken, "So
shall your descendants be." And not being weak in faith, he did
not consider his own body, already dead (since he was about
a hundred years old), and the deadness of Sarah's womb. He
did not waver at the promise of God through unbelief, but was
strengthened in faith, giving glory to God, and being fully convinced
that what He had promised He was also able to perform.

ROMANS 4:18-21

PONDER THIS People with weak faith often have a small view of God. If your faith is weak, you need to get to know God. The Bible says, "And those who know Your name will put their trust in You" (Psalm 9:10a). Glance at your problem, but gaze at your God. Verse 18 says of Abraham, "Who, contrary to hope, in hope believed." Do you think you're hopeless? Do you think God is finished with you or never got started with you? Do you think other people can know God but not you? God sent me here to tell you that God has hope for you.

Abraham looked at God, who can bring life out of death and make something out of nothing, and said, "I am going to believe in that God!" Don't look at yourself or your problems and say you're hopeless. You are not! God can bring life to you, and God will make something out of you. The only thing God makes something out of is nothing, and so if you'll become nothing, He'll make something out of you. It's time you stop relying on yourself and hope in God.

- When have you felt hopeless? How do you respond in these moments?

- What would it look like to turn to God in your hopeless moment?

PRACTICE THIS Tell God about the areas in which you feel hopeless and discouraged. Submit to Him and trust Him with those things.

PRAY OVER THIS

What does it profit, my brethren, if someone says he has faith but
does not have works? Can faith save him? If a brother or sister is
naked and destitute of daily food, and one of you says to them,
"Depart in peace, be warmed and filled," but you do not give
them the things which are needed for the body, what does it
profit? Thus also faith by itself, if it does not have works, is dead.

JAMES 2:14-17

PONDER THIS You are not saved by faith and works, but you are saved by faith
that works. You are justified by faith alone, but the faith that justifies is never
alone; it always has works. If your religion hasn't changed your life, you'd better
change your religion. When God does something in your heart and in your life,
it will be seen. If you say, "Well, I'm trusting Him, but I'm not going to make it
known. I'm not going to take any stand," then you're not really trusting Him.

Faith without works is dead. Walking down the aisle won't save anybody, but
what it indicates will save everybody. Jesus said, "For whoever is ashamed of Me
and My words in this adulterous and sinful generation, of him the Son of Man also
will be ashamed when He comes in the glory of His Father with the holy angels"
(Mark 8:38). You see, faith responds to the guidance of God. Faith is acting on
what we know to be true. We faithfully obey. If you have Paul's faith, you'll have
James' works—they simply go together.

- What are some works that come because of faith?

- When have you struggled to live by faith? What makes this
  difficult?

PRACTICE THIS Read Genesis 22 and observe the ways Abraham displayed his
faith through his works. Pray for God to grow your faith.

PRAY OVER THIS

But someone will say, "You have faith, and I have works. Show me your faith without your works, and I will show you my faith by my works. You believe that there is one God. You do well. Even the demons believe—and tremble! But do you want to know, O foolish man, that faith without works is dead?

JAMES 2:18-20

PONDER THIS Did you know grace is a unique marker of the Christian faith? Jesus Christ has cornered the market on grace. No one else, except our Lord, teaches salvation by grace. There are only two kinds of religion in the world— grace and works. One is spelled *do*, and the other is spelled *done*. We often want to make passages sound contradictory between Paul and James, but there's no real contradiction here. They're heads and tails of the same coin.

In Romans 4, Paul wrote about justification before God. James wrote about justification before men. God knows I am justified when I trust Christ. But you can't see my trust. All you can see is what I say and how I live. Paul was talking about the root of our salvation; James was talking about the fruit of our salvation. The root is beneath the ground; the fruit is hanging out on the tree. But the fruit is the proof of the root.

- What are some fruits of God's work in your life?

- Is the fruit of faith possible without the root? Why or why not?

PRACTICE THIS Encourage a friend about the fruit of faith you see in his or her life.

30

PRAY OVER THIS

"For as the body without the spirit is dead, so
faith without works is dead also."

JAMES 2:26

PONDER THIS What good is a body of truth without the life of the spirit? You may say, "I believe this and this and this." You take all your beliefs and put them together, and you've got a body of truth. But if there's no life in that body of truth, it can't move. The body without the spirit is dead. The body in this illustration is your belief. But if that's all you have, and you don't have the Spirit of God in you, then you have no life. What good is a corpse without a spirit? What good is belief without life?

If a person is dead, what would make that person get up and do good works? Wouldn't he have to have life first? I could fling his arms around and stand him up and make him walk. But what good is that? I'm just manipulating a corpse. Before he can work, he's got to have life. If he received life and began to walk around again, would his walking around give him life? No. He walks around because he has received life. The works don't make him alive. He can't do the works until he gets life. Once he has life, then he has works. And once we have the Spirit, we have life and works.

- How have you seen evidence of your "being alive" because of Jesus?

- Why is it easy to focus on works as the way to get to God?

PRACTICE THIS Write down some of the works you do for God. Consider why you do them and ask God to fill you with His life so that these things are a byproduct of living for Him and not an effort to earn from Him.

PRAY OVER THIS

"These things I have spoken to you, that My joy may
remain in you, and that your joy may be full."

JOHN 15:11

PONDER THIS Christian joy is supernatural in its source, and it is steadfast in its strength. The shortest verse in the Greek is 1 Thessalonians 5:16. It's two words in English, but one word in Greek. The two words in English are these: "Rejoice always." It's the shortest verse, but it deals with the longest time: always. This is the joy Jesus said will remain. It's not happiness. It's joy! You're not supposed to be happy all the time.

Imagine you came home today and everything in your house had been stolen by thieves. Your heirlooms, your treasures, your photo albums—all gone. Would that take away your joy? If it did, those things are the source of your joy. Your joy is no better than its source. You've got to have a source that is better than things for you to have joy that is steadfast. Only the joy of Jesus remains always.

- What are some things that bring you joy? What does that indicate as the source of your joy?

- What would it look like to rejoice always? What sounds good about that? What sounds challenging about that?

PRACTICE THIS Speak to fellow believers about how you can encourage one another to hold onto joy.

32

PRAY OVER THIS

"A new commandment I give to you, that you love one another;
as I have loved you, that you also love one another."

JOHN 13:34

PONDER THIS What is real love? What is Christ-like love? It is selfless love! Selfless love means not being primarily concerned about "number one." And selfless love is real humility. Unbounded love and pride can never dwell in the same heart! Only in pure humility can there be genuine love.

Many times, we excuse ourselves when we're irritable if we're tired or worn out. We've had a hard day. People have mistreated us. And we bark and snap at people and say, "If you knew what I've been through, you'd understand." But Jesus, facing the cross, still showed love. Jesus, knowing that the hour was coming when they would crucify Him, still steadfastly loved them. If your so-called love cannot stand the test of hard times, you don't have real love. If you just love when times are good, any person can do that. But Jesus loved selflessly under extreme pressure.

- What are some excuses you make for not loving people?

- What are some ways you can selflessly love those around you?

PRACTICE THIS Practically love someone in a selfless way today.

PRAY OVER THIS

"Hear, O Israel: The LORD our God, the LORD is one!
You shall love the LORD your God with all your heart,
with all your soul, and with all your strength."

DEUTERONOMY 6:4-5

PONDER THIS What is the foundation for the family? It is love for God. That may sound simplistic, but it is incredibly true and profound. Loving God with a sincere love means with all your heart, moms and dads. If you do not sincerely love God, you don't have much of a chance of having a successful family according to the Bible's standards. As a matter of fact, you have no real chance of having a successful family.

Many kids are turned off because they see that their parents profess religion, but they don't love God with all their hearts. We're to love God with a sincere love. We're to love God with a selfless love. We're to love God with all our souls. Kids are looking for parents who have such integrity that there is nothing in their lives marked off as private from God. Kids want to see parents who bring God into their family, recreation, business, and their marital relationship. This is a sincere love, a selfless love, and a strong love.

- What foundation was your family built on? How did that affect your upbringing?

- How would your life change if you were to love God with all your heart, soul, and strength?

PRACTICE THIS Pray that God would grow your love for Him and help you share that love with others.

PRAY OVER THIS

"You shall teach them diligently to your children, and shall talk of them when you sit in your house, when you walk by the way, when you lie down, and when you rise up."

DEUTERONOMY 6:7

PONDER THIS Children have a way of discerning who is real and who is a phony. My children know their daddy is not perfect, but none of my children will say their dad is a phony. And they know their momma is not a phony. They know we have our faults, but they know we love God with all our hearts. It should be a genuine love that you have for God that you share with the next generation.

The problem in so many of our homes is that we suddenly get on a religious ritual and regimen and decide our kids are going to learn the Bible. We say, "You sit still while I instill." That's not the way God's Word is to be taught. God's Word is to be taught creatively—when you go in and out of the house, when you wake up in the morning, and when you go to bed at night. You're to be constantly teaching the Word of God. How do you do it? Sure, there's to be a set time of Bible reading, but it can also be a natural conversation throughout your life. It can be fun and creative. Just do it diligently—here a little, there a little, line upon line, precept upon precept. It's not easy, but the cumulative force is so impactful.

- What are some creative ways you were taught the Bible?

- Who can you teach the Word of God to...a little bit at a time?

PRACTICE THIS Think about the people you have the opportunity to influence with the love and hope of Christ. What are some things they are interested in? What are some creative avenues of sharing God's truth that may be effective for them?

PRAY OVER THIS

"You shall bind them as a sign on your hand, and they shall
be as frontlets between your eyes. You shall write them
on the doorposts of your house and on your gates."

DEUTERONOMY 6:8-9

PONDER THIS Be careful what you say. Talk about the Word of God. Apply the Bible to life situations and teach the Word of God conspicuously. *Conspicuously* means "in a clearly visible way." The Jews had little boxes they call phylacteries, and they would tie a portion of the Word of God to their hands and put some right between their eyes, on their foreheads. They took this literally. There's certainly nothing wrong with that, but I think there's a far deeper meaning. The Word of God between your eyes means whatever you think is to be controlled by the Word of God. The Word of God on your hand means whatever you do is to be controlled by the Word of God.

Simply put, the Word of God is to be very evident in your life. Verse 9 says, "You shall write them on the doorposts of your house and on your gates." Your house ought to have scriptural mottos. The Word of God is to impact everything—the atmosphere of your home, the way you interact in a hard conversation, the way you give generously. It is always to be on your mind and in your hand.

- What is an area of your life that may not point to Jesus?

- Do you desire to be mindful of God's Word? If so, how is that evident in your life? If not, what needs to change?

PRACTICE THIS Find a practical way to keep God's Word before you throughout your day today.

PRAY OVER THIS

Let your speech always be with grace, seasoned with salt,
that you may know how you ought to answer each one.

COLOSSIANS 4:6

PONDER THIS Salt has many different purposes. One is adding taste to food. And grace adds flavor to speech. Salt is a preservative, and speech that issues out of the nature of grace will preserve relationships. "Let your speech always be with grace." Do you know what grace is? Grace is not giving people what they deserve; grace is giving them what they need. You say, "My wife doesn't deserve that kind of speech," or "My husband doesn't deserve those words," but that's more reason to speak with grace because the other person needs it.

Do you know why we can't be intimate? Because we're afraid to expose ourselves. We're afraid we'll get criticized. If I expose my inadequacy, then I'm afraid I won't be accepted. Out of acceptance grows trust. And then out of trust, there comes intimacy. And so, you see, intimacy can only grow where there is a place of safety. Grace gives space for safety, and it builds bridges instead of tearing them down.

- When has someone extended grace to you when you did not deserve it?

- What would it look like to extend grace to the people around you? What makes that difficult?

PRACTICE THIS Consider a recent conflict you were in. How did you act at that moment? How might you have responded more graciously?

PRAY OVER THIS

So then, my beloved brethren, let every man be
swift to hear, slow to speak, slow to wrath.

JAMES 1:19

PONDER THIS Why do we retreat in the face of conflict? Several reasons. Sometimes we fear the anger of another, so we just close up. Sometimes we may think, "If I don't retreat, our relationship will be broken." Sometimes, and I suppose this is the most insidious of all, we retreat because we're afraid that if we get into an argument and a discussion, we will have to admit something about ourselves. We might have to see where we are wrong, and so we just retreat.

But unresolved conflict is not resolved by retreating; it only gets worse. You may stuff it down, you may repress it, but I will guarantee your stomach will keep the score. If you have a problem that you shove out the front door and refuse to address, it will crawl around the house and come in the basement window. Don't practice avoidance. Love others enough to confront. The ability to confront reveals the strength of a relationship. Good communication in relationships begins with listening.

- Who are you frequently in conflict with? How do you typically handle conflict with that person?

- Why do you think we often struggle with listening during conflict?

PRACTICE THIS Share with a friend the reasons you struggle to listen during conflict. Think together about strategies to help you remember to listen amid conflict.

PRAY OVER THIS

And the Lord God said, "It is not good that man should be alone; I will make him a helper comparable to him." Out of the ground the Lord God formed every beast of the field and every bird of the air, and brought them to Adam to see what he would call them. And whatever Adam called each living creature, that was its name.

GENESIS 2:18-19

PONDER THIS God's plan for marriage is one plus one equals one. "Two... become one flesh" (Matthew 19:5), and "What God has joined together, let not man separate" (Matthew 19:6). The Bible says, "And they were both naked...and were not ashamed" (Genesis 2:25). What does that mean? It means they were so unified that there was no shame and no intimidation. They were willing and able to share everything.

There is no way you can win in a war with your mate. Why? Because you and your mate are one. And if you damage him or her, you don't win, you lose. You are one flesh. A man at war with his wife is at war with himself. Any woman at war with her husband is at war with herself. Jesus alone can build the homes we need. Jesus is the greatest home builder; Satan is the greatest home wrecker.

- When were you determined to win an argument? How did you conduct yourself at that time?

- When did you work through a conflict? What was good about that? What was difficult about that?

PRACTICE THIS Pray and ask God to help you work through conflict in a way that makes much of Him and His grace.

PRAY OVER THIS

Now when they had gone through Phrygia and the region of
Galatia, they were forbidden by the Holy Spirit to preach the
word in Asia. After they had come to Mysia, they tried to go into
Bithynia, but the Spirit did not permit them. So passing by Mysia,
they came down to Troas. And a vision appeared to Paul in the
night. A man of Macedonia stood and pleaded with him, saying,
"Come over to Macedonia and help us." Now after he had seen the
vision, immediately we sought to go to Macedonia, concluding
that the Lord had called us to preach the gospel to them.

ACTS 16:6-10

PONDER THIS Have you ever tried to teach someone else to drive a car? What's
the first thing you show that person: the accelerator or the brake? You show him
the brake, and if he says, "I'm not interested in the brake," you probably say, "Give
me the keys back." Those of us who know how to drive know how important
the brake is. Before God will ever show you the accelerator, He must show you
the brake. If you're not interested in the restraint of the Spirit, you'll never know
the release of the Spirit. The path of life is strewn with the wrecks of people who
have high-powered engines and faulty brakes. They don't know how to listen to
God's "No." God's "No" is as important as God's "Go." Someone said, "A fanatic is
somebody who, having lost sight of his goal, increases his speed." Do you know
the restraint of the Spirit? Can God say "no" to you, and you listen?

- When have you sensed the Spirit telling you "No" about
  something you really wanted? How did you respond?

- How often do you ask God, with sincere openness, what He
  would have you do?

PRACTICE THIS Ask for God's direction in the matters of your life.

PRAY OVER THIS

Wisdom calls aloud outside; she raises her voice in the
open squares. She cries out in the chief concourses, at the
openings of the gates in the city she speaks her words: "How
long, you simple ones, will you love simplicity? For scorners
delight in their scorning, and fools hate knowledge."

PROVERBS 1:20-22

PONDER THIS On a reality TV show, a man stepped on an elevator and noticed everybody was facing the back wall; nobody was facing the door, even though there was no opening in the back wall. The man got on the elevator, looked around, surveyed the situation, and began to face the back wall as the elevator went up and down.

This shows the power of peer pressure, public opinion, and our desire to conform to what other people are doing. What do we do about this? We guard our company. Let your home be the happiest place on Earth. Let your children know you love them and that you love their friends, but at the same time, you are watching the company they keep. What we expect of our children should be a reality in our lives, too. May we guard our company and be aware of those who may influence us more than we realize.

- What are some ways we face peer pressure as adults?

- How can we seek to be most influenced by God's Word?

PRACTICE THIS Send an encouraging, welcoming message to a teen or young adult God has placed in your life. Consider how you can get to know that teen and his or her peers.

PRAY OVER THIS

Now to Him who is able to do exceedingly abundantly above all that we
ask or think, according to the power that works in us, to Him be glory
in the church by Christ Jesus to all generations, forever and ever. Amen.

EPHESIANS 3:20-21

PONDER THIS There was a pastor I knew who said, "You know, God never did give
me anything I ever wanted." Right away, that sounds kind of strange because
this was a man who served God all his life and had a fruitful ministry. He went on,
"God didn't let me go to the college I wanted to go to. God never let me pastor
the church I wanted to pastor. God didn't even let me marry the woman I wanted
to marry." His wife is sitting right there. You talk about a guy who was digging a
hole deeper and deeper. But then he gave a big smile and said, "God never did
give me anything I ever wanted, but He always gave me something better than I
ever wanted." Isn't that beautiful?

God didn't give us what we wanted; God gave us something better than we
wanted. Paul wanted to go to Bithynia and into Asia, but the Holy Spirit said, "I
want you to go over to Greece. I want you to go over to Macedonia." (See Acts 16:6-
10.) And God opened up all of Europe for the preaching of the Gospel because He
was supernaturally building His Church.

- When has God worked differently than you expected?

- When do you struggle to trust what God has for you? How can
  you trust Him more?

PRACTICE THIS Pray and ask God to help you trust Him in the areas where His
plans for you are different (and better) than yours.

42

PRAY OVER THIS

But if we walk in the light as He is in the light, we
have fellowship with one another, and the blood of
Jesus Christ His Son cleanses us from all sin.

1 JOHN 1:7

PONDER THIS What is our fellowship? It is in the Gospel of our Lord and Savior Jesus Christ. What is the bond that holds us together? We have a common Lord, a common life, a common love, and that's what makes the fellowship of the Church what it is.

I used to play football. When we would win a big game, the people up in the stands—your dad and mom, and friends—would hug and say, "We won, we won!" and the coaches down there would embrace and say, "We won, we won."
And while they took joy in the win, they didn't actually play the game. I've been so tired I couldn't even lift my hands to pull my jersey off. It'd be wet and sweaty, and my arms would be bruised, but I'd finally get that jersey over my head, unlace those shoes, and rip that tape off my ankles. As I'd sit there with another guy who's bruised and battered, who's been down there in the trenches with me, I would look over at him and say, "Bill, we won, didn't we?" That's fellowship: when you've been in the trenches together.

- What would it look like to be in the trenches of faith together with others in the Church?

- In what ways do you seek fellowship with believers around you? What is difficult for you about living in fellowship with others?

PRACTICE THIS Share a meal with some fellow believers and encourage them about the moments you have been supported by the fellowship you have in Christ.

43

PRAY OVER THIS

The proverbs of Solomon the son of David, king of Israel: to know wisdom and instruction, to perceive the words of understanding, to receive the instruction of wisdom, justice, judgment, and equity; to give prudence to the simple, to the young man knowledge and discretion.

PROVERBS 1:1-4

PONDER THIS A wise man can look down the pike: he can prepare for the future; he can see danger; and he can get out of the way. But this is not true for the simple-minded. I don't mean that he is stupid; he just cannot think about danger. That's the reason a teenager is so likely to hurt himself after drinking beer and driving 60, 70, or 80 miles per hour. He just can't see the danger; he can't think ahead.

But how can this tragedy be avoided? What should we do with the simple-minded? You, parent, need to read the Word daily. It needs to be real in your life. You need to be changed by the Word and then read it with your children and explain it to them. You start with the simple when he is young. God has given the Bible for your change and growth, and God has given you to teach your child. One of the chief ways the simple learn is by example. Your child is open, and whatever example is set before him or her makes a great impression.

- What are some examples your parents left for you? How did you learn from them?

- What is your rhythm of reading the Word and spending time with God? Is it something you would consider a good example for someone else? Why or why not?

PRACTICE THIS Talk to someone you know who looks up to you and ask what that person has learned from you.

PRAY OVER THIS

At that time the disciples came to Jesus, saying, "Who then is greatest in the kingdom of heaven?" Then Jesus called a little child to Him, set him in the midst of them, and said, "Assuredly, I say to you, unless you are converted and become as little children, you will by no means enter the kingdom of heaven. Therefore whoever humbles himself as this little child is the greatest in the kingdom of heaven. Whoever receives one little child like this in My name receives Me."

MATTHEW 18:1-5

PONDER THIS What is the word you hear from a little child so often? *"Why?"* Don't despise children when they ask that. What a golden opportunity that they're asking you why.

When we become adults, it's so hard to break through that abominable pride. That's the reason the Lord Jesus spoke the words from today's passage to adults. Sometimes a child will come forward and give his or her heart to the Lord Jesus Christ, and some well-meaning counselor will get that little child and ask a lot of adult questions. And if the little child can't answer the adult questions, the counselor will say the little child is not ready. That's backward. It's not that the little child must become like the adult; the adult must become like a little child. Children have an incredible trust factor. That's not bad—it's wonderful. That is the way God intended it. They believe fully in Him.

- How have you seen the simplicity of faith in a child?

- Why is it so difficult for adults to have child-like faith?

PRACTICE THIS Ask God to develop a child-like faith in you.

45

Train up a child in the way he should go, and
when he is old he will not depart from it.

PROVERBS 22:6

PONDER THIS God never makes copies; He only makes originals. And every one of us has those little idiosyncrasies and things that God has put into us. Your child comes with a certain collection of genes, talents, and abilities that can grow into spiritual gifts. You are wise as a parent if you look at that child and see the way he or she should go.

If you tried to bend the trunk of a mighty oak, you couldn't do it. But if you take the mighty oak when it's just starting as a little branch or twig, you can bend it. That's what God is saying, "There is a way the child should go." We must train them while they are young, and we need to study them as individuals. Children are different. God has wired them differently and gifted them all in different ways to be used for His glory.

- What were some ways you were trained as a child? How did that help you?

- How has God uniquely wired you? Who was an adult who understood your unique qualities?

PRACTICE THIS Think about those you know in the next generation. What are some gifts they have that are unique? Spend some time getting to know how God uniquely wired them.

PRAY OVER THIS

By faith Noah, being divinely warned of things not yet seen,
moved with godly fear, prepared an ark for the saving of his
household, by which he condemned the world and became
heir of the righteousness which is according to faith.

HEBREWS 11:7

PONDER THIS If you remember enough of your high school English studies, you know what a preposition is. There are three key prepositions in Ephesians 2:8-10: by, through, and for. It is "*by* grace," "*through* faith," and "*for* good works."

Genesis 6:8 says, "Noah found grace in the eyes of the LORD." Did you know this is the first mention of grace in the Bible? How did Noah and his kids get saved? By grace! And what is grace? Grace is God's incredible, indescribable love that leads God to love us when we don't deserve it: "while we were still sinners, Christ died for us" (Romans 5:8b). We have a covenant of grace. We're not saved by good works. We're not saved by joining a church, giving our money, getting baptized, obeying the Ten Commandments, or living right. Salvation is not a reward for the righteous; it is a gift for the guilty. Noah was not saved because he was such a good guy; he was saved by the grace of God.

If you are in Christ, God has worked through these same powerful prepositions in your life.

- How has God worked through powerful prepositions in your life?

- Why are grace and faith so important in your walk with Christ?

PRACTICE THIS Praise God that salvation comes by faith and not through good works.

47

PRAY OVER THIS

And behold, I Myself am bringing floodwaters on the earth, to
destroy from under heaven all flesh in which is the breath of
life; everything that is on the earth shall die. But I will establish
My covenant with you; and you shall go into the ark—you, your
sons, your wife, and your sons' wives with you. And of every living
thing of all flesh you shall bring two of every sort into the ark,
to keep them alive with you; they shall be male and female.

GENESIS 6:17-19

PONDER THIS Many folks just believe they're kept saved by just holding on. I hear some people say, "Pray for me, that I'll hold out faithful to the end." Suppose God had said to Noah, "Noah, if you want to be saved, you put some pegs on the outside of that ark. When it starts to rain, you get on a step ladder and go up and hold onto those pegs. Your feet will be dangling; the water will be rising; and it's going to be rough. But Noah, if you can hold onto those pegs until the water goes down, you'll be saved." I don't think Noah would have made it, do you? I can only imagine Noah saying, "Pray for me, that I'll hold out faithful to the end."

That's the kind of salvation some people think they have. They think they're saved by holding onto God. No way! We're saved because He holds onto us! And He says, "No one is able to snatch them out of My Father's hand" (John 10:29). Noah was shut into that ship. Some believe they're going to get eternal security one day when they go to Heaven. They believe they're going to step into Heaven, slam the door behind them, and say, "Whew, I made it. Hallelujah! I'm safe now." May I tell you that security is not in a place? Security is in a person, and His name is Jesus.

- When have you tried to work hard for your faith? What happened?

- What difference does it make whether we are holding onto God or He is holding onto us?

PRACTICE THIS Pray that you would find your ultimate security in Jesus alone.

48

PRAY OVER THIS

But God demonstrates His own love toward us, in that
while we were still sinners, Christ died for us.

ROMANS 5:8

PONDER THIS Many of you would say, "Pastor, my heart is breaking because my son, my daughter, may not be a fool, but my son, my daughter, is a smart aleck. What do you do with a child like that?" Well, first of all, remember that scolding and lecturing a scorner does very little good. If you think you can sit down your know-it-all child and preach to him, you've got another thought coming. You're not going to be able to drill it into his head. Scolding is going to do little good. As a matter of fact, it'll probably increase his ability to sin. You need to talk less and pray more. And love that scorner more, then wait for the open door. Not the rebuke, but the open door.

When you've got a rebellious teenager, you surround that child with your love. Let her know where you stand on these issues, but don't constantly be against her. Do not constantly be rebuking her, but be loving, praying, and waiting. Asking, "Oh, God, help me to speak a word in due season." And as you pray, God will work according to His will and ways.

- When have you been tempted to lecture instead of love?

- When has an act of love by another impacted you?

PRACTICE THIS Pray for someone you know to grow in love for the Lord.

49

"The LORD has appeared of old to me, saying: 'Yes,
I have loved you with an everlasting love; therefore
with lovingkindness I have drawn you.'"

JEREMIAH 31:3

PONDER THIS God created Adam and Eve, and He gave them everything they needed. No one can say He didn't raise them right. No one can say He didn't love them. No one can say He didn't spend time with them. No one can say He did not carefully teach them. And He warned them that their future depended on their choices, yet they did wrong. By their own choices and free will, they rebelled against their loving Father.

You can be a good parent and lose a child. But reading the Bible, you're going to see that God is in the same place you are. God is agonizingly watching your children hurt themselves and hurt others, and yet God refuses to step in and storm their control center and make them machines. He won't do it. I'm going to tell you something else: He won't do it with you either. God is looking down from Heaven right now at some grown rebellious children, and He's stretching out His hands in love and saying, "Come to Me."

- Who do you know who has rebelled against God? How does that make you feel? How does it feel to know God empathizes with the hurt you experience in these moments?

- Who in your life is far from God? How can you extend love to that person?

PRACTICE THIS Take a step toward loving someone who's far from God.

PRAY OVER THIS

There is neither Jew nor Greek, there is neither slave nor free, there
is neither male nor female; for you are all one in Christ Jesus.

GALATIANS 3:28

PONDER THIS I want to tell you something about my wife, Joyce. I love her with all my heart, but she knows she's not first in my life. She knows God is first in my life. And she doesn't mind being second. Now, she's first among all human beings, but she's second in my life. She knows I can love her more by putting her second than I ever could by putting her first. And I know I'm not first in Joyce's life. I know I'm second; I don't mind that because she loves me with a love that she could not love me with had she not fortified her faith in the Lord. In 1 Peter 3:7, the Bible speaks of us "as being heirs together of the grace of life." What does it mean to be heirs together? That's joint heirs. That means share-and-share-alike. There's no male superiority and female inferiority when it comes to trusting in God.

The spiritual oneness Joyce and I have is oneness in Christ Jesus. I'm a male and she's a female, but we are one in the Lord Jesus Christ. I say without stutter, stammer, or apology, the secret of our home is God Himself.

- What would it look like to put God first in your life? What would change? What would stay the same?

- How does having the Lord as the first priority in your life affect the way you love your spouse and others?

PRACTICE THIS Ask God to reveal any priorities that do not honor Him.

PRAY OVER THIS

Rejoice always, pray without ceasing, in everything give
thanks; for this is the will of God in Christ Jesus for you.

1 THESSALONIANS 5:16-18

PONDER THIS Prayer is so important in marriage. We've tried to do it from the first day we got married. We pray for our children and our grandchildren, every day by name, lifting them up to the Lord because the Bible says, "Unless the LORD builds the house, they labor in vain who build it; unless the LORD guards the city, the watchman stays awake in vain" (Psalm 127:1). As I look back on the life God has given us, I would be a sheer fool, an unmitigated egomaniac, if I tried to take praise for what God has done. God answers prayer.

Some men don't want to pray with women because they have a hard outer shell, but guys, humble yourselves, practice prayer with your wives. Let her hear you praying; let her hear you pouring out your heart before God. It will give her great confidence and great comfort. It will bring you closer to God and closer to one another.

- When do you regularly pray? What would it look like to pray without ceasing?

- What are some things that keep us from praying without ceasing? What can we do about those hindrances?

PRACTICE THIS Set up a reminder for regular prayer in a place where you will see it daily, such AS on your mirror or at your sink.

52

For this reason a man shall leave his father and mother and
be joined to his wife, and the two shall become one flesh;'
so then they are no longer two, but one flesh. Therefore
what God has joined together, let not man separate.

MARK 10:7-9

PONDER THIS Our spirit is that part of our nature that truly makes us in the image of God, for the Bible says God is Spirit. (See John 4:24.) And with our spirit, we have spiritual relationships. We know God through the spirit. The Bible says when we get saved, God's Spirit bears witness with our spirit that we're children of God. (See Romans 8:16.) You are body, soul, and spirit. When your body is right, you're healthy. When your soul is right, you're happy. When your spirit is right, you're holy. And God wants you to be healthy, happy, and holy. Now what does that have to do with marriage?

Well, you need to understand who's getting married. A body, soul, and spirit is marrying another body, soul, and spirit. Here is what God is saying: They are no longer two but become one flesh. God's math is one plus one equals one. But how are you to be one? You're to be one physically, one psychologically, and one spiritually. There's to be the union of your bodies because you are a body. There's to be the union of your souls because you are a soul. And there's to be the union of your spirit because you are a spirit.

- Why is it important to understand ourselves as soul, spirit, and body?

- Are there married couples you admire? How do they reflect oneness in their relationships?

PRACTICE THIS Pray for the married couples you know to be strengthened in unity in body, soul, and spirit.

PRAY OVER THIS

In this is love, not that we loved God, but that He loved us
and sent His Son to be the propitiation for our sins. Beloved,
if God so loved us, we also ought to love one another

1 JOHN 4:10-11

PONDER THIS When you were dating, you likely had a list of desires in another person. You thought, "I want somebody good-looking or beautiful. I want somebody who thinks I'm funny. I want somebody with a good personality. I want somebody with certain physical attributes and perhaps certain intellectual gifts; somebody who can make me feel good." And the time comes when you finally say to that young lady or that young man, "I love you." That may be true, but some people say this to mean, "I want you because you meet a particular need in my life." That kind of love is not the love God is talking about that binds husbands and wives together. As a matter of fact, that kind of love is very conditional. And if those are the reasons you got married—because of somebody's charm or beauty—then your marriage is in danger. Now I'm not saying charm, wit, and beauty are not important, but those things fade.

Can you see how dangerous that kind of conditional love is to a marriage? It is rooted in self. God calls us to more.

- What is the difference between unconditional love and conditional love?

- What are some ways we tend to love people conditionally?

PRACTICE THIS Thank someone who has shown you unconditional love.

54

PRAY OVER THIS

If it is possible, as much as depends on you, live
peaceably with all men.

ROMANS 12:18

PONDER THIS God's love for us is unconditional. And when the Bible says a husband is to love his wife, God means agape love, which is unconditional. Think about the value of spouses who love one another without condition. You have security in the place of fear. You have peace, which replaces guilt. You have joy that replaces anger.

Some couples reason: It would be better for our children if we got a divorce than for our children to live in this constant fighting. Sociologists have told us divorce is seldom, if ever, a positive factor in the life of a child. If you're really talking about what is better for the child, I suggest you go ask the children and see what they think about it. You say, "Well, the only two alternatives we have are divorce or constant fighting." There's a third alternative: You get your heart right with God, and you stop fighting and don't seek to excuse it. The Bible says we're to live peaceably with all people. This certainly includes our marriages.

- What are some of the fights you have most frequently with your spouse? How do you handle those conflicts?

- What are some things that make it difficult to live in peace with others? How can God help you overcome those things?

PRACTICE THIS Ask God to help you to live at peace with everyone.

PRAY OVER THIS

Let nothing be done through selfish ambition or conceit,
but in lowliness of mind let each esteem others better
than himself. Let each of you look out not only for his
own interests, but also for the interests of others.

PHILIPPIANS 2:3-4

PONDER THIS Do you know what most of our arguments are? Ego against ego! Self against self! Before long, there's going to be a war between those two kingdoms. The husband needs to step down from the throne of his life and enthrone King Jesus. The same is true for the wife!

How many kingdoms are there? There is just one kingdom—Jesus rules both thrones. And here's a wonderful secret: The Jesus in the husband is not going to fight the Jesus in the wife. If Christ is on the throne of both lives, the husband and wife will be one spiritually. You're going to be able to pray together and worship together. Because you're one spiritually, is it easier to be one psychologically? Not always! Where is the problem psychologically? Why can't we heal our arguments? Because of our egos. But when we take ourselves off the throne and enthrone Christ, we can solve those problems. There are no problems too big to solve; just people too small to solve them.

- When has your ego affected an argument in which you were involved?

- How can you get past your ego? What makes that so difficult?

PRACTICE THIS Pray and repent for the ways your ego has hurt your relationships with others.

PRAY OVER THIS

For this is the will of God, your sanctification: that you should abstain from sexual immorality; that each of you should know how to possess his own vessel in sanctification and honor, not in passion of lust, like the Gentiles who do not know God.

1 THESSALONIANS 4:3-5

PONDER THIS Intimacy in marriage is a form of communication. It's a way of knowing someone. It's a way of saying, "I love you" that cannot be put into words. It's very beautiful. Sometimes we have been taught to think of sex as dirty or impure. Outside the bonds of matrimony, it is. But inside the bonds of matrimony, it's pure and wonderful. So, when the Bible says, "You shall not commit adultery" (Exodus 20:14), or "Flee sexual immorality" (1 Corinthians 6:18a), it's important to understand God is not trying to keep sex *from* you; God is keeping sex *for* you.

In my office, I have a picture on the wall. It's an ordinary picture: if someone stole it, there'd be no great loss, and if it got damaged, there'd be no great problem. But if it were a Rembrandt, a Van Gogh, or something like that, it would probably be in a vault because it would be so valuable. I wouldn't want it marred, misused, or abused. When God puts these high walls around sex, it's because it is so valuable. And God wants us to cherish it as His special gift.

- What were you taught about sex as a child? How has that affected you as an adult?

- How do you treat something when it is valuable to you?

PRACTICE THIS Thank God for making valuable things and ask Him to help you prize the things He values.

57

PRAY OVER THIS

For we all stumble in many things. If anyone does not stumble
in word, he is a perfect man, able also to bridle the whole body.
Indeed, we put bits in horses' mouths that they may obey us, and
we turn their whole body. Look also at ships: although they are
so large and are driven by fierce winds, they are turned by a very
small rudder wherever the pilot desires. Even so, the tongue is a
little member and boasts great things. See how great a forest a
little fire kindles! And the tongue is a fire, a world of iniquity. The
tongue is so set among our members that it defiles the whole body,
and sets on fire the course of nature; and it is set on fire by hell.

JAMES 3:2-6

PONDER THIS Just as the horse is controlled by the bit and the ship is controlled
by the rudder, your words give direction to your home. If you don't like the way
your marriage is headed, you'd better watch your words. Your words can bring
your ship into a safe harbor, or it can put it on the rocks. Not only does James say
the tongue brings direction, but he also says the tongue may bring destruction.
Look back at verse 6. If you have a torch tongue, you can burn down your marriage.
Fire is a wonderful servant, but it's a poor master. Words can warm a heart or
burn down a home. The tongue may bring destruction. The tongue may bring
defilement. You can poison your marriage with your tongue. Our words matter:
They can be so destructive if we let them go out of the control of God. Our words
are formative: They can give direction to our families. This is why we are to trust
God with even the small details of words.

- When was the last time you said something that hurt someone
  else? What do you need to do considering today's passage?

- What are some words of encouragement your family may need?

PRACTICE THIS Encourage and uplift members of your family today with a
meaningful text, note, or conversation.

PRAY OVER THIS

Then I went down to the potter's house, and there he was, making something at the wheel. And the vessel that he made of clay was marred in the hand of the potter; so he made it again into another vessel, as it seemed good to the potter to make. Then the word of the LORD came to me, saying: "O house of Israel, can I not do with you as this potter?" says the LORD. "Look, as the clay is in the potter's hand, so are you in My hand, O house of Israel!"

JEREMIAH 18:3-6

PONDER THIS Imagine a forest fire sweeping through an area that comes across a stump primed for burning. The fire comes sweeping along, and the stump has rosin and pine tar on it, so it burns brightly. And then it goes out. Then, maybe the underbrush grows up again in three or four years and another fire comes along, burning furiously. When it gets to that stump, it may ignite it again, but it doesn't burn nearly as brightly, not nearly as long, and the fire goes out. There may come a time in later years when the fire roars and comes through, but when it comes to that blackened and charred stump, it doesn't even glow. The fire jumps right over. That happens in congregations, too.

I have been preaching when the power of God's Spirit would move across the congregation like a fire, and souls would come forward weeping, saying, "I want to give my heart to Jesus Christ." But some will sit there untouched. They don't feel a thing. The fire of God's Spirit never moves on them. They have eyes, but they don't see. They have ears, but they don't hear. I want to beg of you: While the clay is soft and pliable, come to Him, even if you've messed up, and He will receive you.

- What are some things that lead you to grow cold toward God?

- When was a time you had a passion and desire for God? What happened? What is different now?

PRACTICE THIS Pray and ask God to fill you with His Spirit and a passion to know Him more.

PRAY OVER THIS

Moreover if your brother sins against you, go and
tell him his fault between you and him alone. If he
hears you, you have gained your brother.

MATTHEW 18:15

PONDER THIS We shame God the Father when we don't get along as brothers and sisters. It disgraces Him. It also discourages the faithful. There's nothing worse than being in a church where there's no harmony, and there's nothing sweeter than being in a church where there is harmony. "Behold, how good and how pleasant it is for brethren to dwell together in unity!" (Psalm 133:1). Our Lord Jesus, in John 17:21b, said, "that they also may be one in Us, that the world may believe that You sent Me." Did you know our unity is a form of evangelism? It tells the world we are Jesus' Church because we have reconciliation and peace with one another. Outside of God, profound peace with one another is not possible. We may be able to get along when we are only talking on the surface, but as soon as we become close to one another, we find conflict. Reconciliation is only possible through Christ.

Satan loves to see brothers and sisters who cannot get along. The cause of Christ is hurt more by church squabbles and fusses than by false doctrine. This is a perplexing problem that can only be resolved in Christ.

- Is there anyone in the Church you are not at peace with? How can you pray for that person? What can you do to live in peace?

- What are some arguments you have had with people in the Church? How have you sought to resolve them?

PRACTICE THIS Take a step toward reconciliation with someone you are at odds with, whether by praying for that person or seeking counsel about how to reconcile.

60

PRAY OVER THIS

Who is he who overcomes the world, but he who believes that
Jesus is the Son of God? This is He who came by water and
blood—Jesus Christ; not only by water, but by water and blood.
And it is the Spirit who bears witness, because the Spirit is truth.
For there are three that bear witness in heaven: the Father,
the Word, and the Holy Spirit; and these three are one.

1 JOHN 5:5-7

PONDER THIS Only Jesus has the answer to the things that really matter. Only Jesus can meet the deepest hunger of the human heart. Only Jesus is the answer to man's sin. Only Jesus gives meaning to life and death. Only Jesus can take the sting out of sin, the gloom out of the grave, and the pain out of parting, and give hope that is steadfast and sure. "To whom shall we go?" (John 6:68b). He alone has the answers to life and death.

But that brings a question: How do we know that Jesus is who we say He is? Why do we believe in Jesus? Why have I given my life to Him? Why do I serve Him? Why would I be willing to die for Him if necessary?

First, the Holy Spirit said to me, "He is the Son of God." And once I received Him into my heart, now I have the witness in myself. You could argue with me all day long and never convince me against Jesus Christ. You could bring sophisticated arguments to me, but I have the witness on the inside. And a Christian with the witness in his heart is never at the mercy of a man with an argument in his mouth.

- How have you seen Jesus satisfy the hunger in someone's heart?

- What are some things that encourage you about having this inner witness as a Christian?

PRACTICE THIS Take time to praise God for giving His Spirit as a witness, comforter, and guide so that we never walk alone.

PRAY OVER THIS

Then Peter came to Him and said, "Lord, how often shall my brother sin against me, and I forgive him? Up to seven times?" Jesus said to him, "I do not say to you, up to seven times, but up to seventy times seven."

MATTHEW 18:21-22

PONDER THIS Scripture says we should forgive not seven times but seventy times seven. That's a very interesting thing because the truth of the matter is, if you truly forgive another person one time, then that sin is gone—it is dissolved, obliterated. You forgive him or her the next time, and that sin is gone, forgiven, obliterated, buried in the grave of God's forgetfulness. If that is true, you're not keeping a record, so every time you forgive that person, it's really the first time; it's not the seventh time or the eighth time because the other times don't count. You're not keeping score, because love does not keep a record: you forgive freely.

You also forgive fully. If you go to a person and ask for forgiveness, make sure it's forgiveness that you get because a proud person will say, "That didn't matter. Forget it." Say, "No, I want you to forgive me." Don't just take a shrug and someone saying it doesn't matter. It does matter for your sake and for the other's sake that there be some closure. Forgetting comes because of forgiveness, and there can be no forgetting until the slate is clean. You can't be sloppy when it comes to getting forgiveness.

Forgive freely, forgive fully, and forgive finally. Bury the offense in the grave of God's forgetfulness. We are to forgive one another even as God, for Christ's sake, has forgiven us.

- When have you struggled to forgive someone else?

- What are some things you need to let go of and forget?

PRACTICE THIS Take a step toward forgiving someone who has wronged you.

PRAY OVER THIS

Now all things are of God, who has reconciled us to Himself
through Jesus Christ, and has given us the ministry of
reconciliation, that is, that God was in Christ reconciling the
world to Himself, not imputing their trespasses to them, and has
committed to us the word of reconciliation. Now then, we are
ambassadors for Christ, as though God were pleading through
us: we implore you on Christ's behalf, be reconciled to God.

2 CORINTHIANS 5:18-20

PONDER THIS One man said he was so distressed with evil in the world that
he got to talking with God and asked, "God, why don't you destroy these evil
people?" And God said, "Alright, I will. I'll start with you." All of us, even the best of
us, fail. A church is not a museum of saints; it's a hospital for sinners. If somebody
has sinned against you, don't make it a matter of gossip. Don't come and tell your
pastor what some church member has done wrong. Go to that individual. Pray.
Go lovingly, humbly, gently, and try to win your brother. If he won't hear you, get
a few trusted friends—spiritually mature people—and go back. If he won't hear
them, then bring it to the church, and the church must confront. If he doesn't
hear the church, it would break our hearts, but we would have to treat him as
though he's never met and known the Lord and Savior Jesus Christ. Attempt,
with all your heart, to win them with the love of Christ.

- With whom do you need to pursue reconciliation?

- Why do you think it is easier to see the sin in others than to see
  the sin in ourselves?

PRACTICE THIS Pray for reconciliation in your broken relationships.

PRAY OVER THIS

Then Jesus said to the twelve, "Do you also want to go away?"
But Simon Peter answered Him, 'Lord, to whom shall we go?
You have the words of eternal life. Also we have come to believe
and know that You are the Christ, the Son of the living God.

JOHN 6:67-69

PONDER THIS I flew on an airplane, and I had to trust the pilot. I ate in a restaurant, and I had to trust the cook. If you read a map, you trust the map maker. What am I saying? I'm saying we trust people every day. "If we receive the witness of men, the witness of God is greater" (1 John 5:9a). And the word "if" there may be translated "since." Since we receive the witness of men, the witness of God is greater.

If you want to know who Jesus Christ is, ask the Holy Spirit. God doesn't just say, "You must believe, and if you can't believe, that's your hard luck." God says, "If you want to believe, I will help you understand and know these things are true." No one can tell me you cannot believe. You may refuse to believe, but I will tell you this: If you want to believe in Jesus Christ and you seek truth, God the Holy Spirit will speak to you and confirm to you that Jesus is the Christ, the Son of the living God. He witnesses to you, and then He witnesses in you.

- What are some things you need to ask God to help you believe?
- When have you asked God to help you believe His truth?

PRACTICE THIS Pray and ask God to help you believe Him through the power of the Holy Spirit.

PRAY OVER THIS

But be doers of the word, and not hearers only, deceiving yourselves. For if anyone is a hearer of the word and not a doer, he is like a man observing his natural face in a mirror; for he observes himself, goes away, and immediately forgets what kind of man he was. But he who looks into the perfect law of liberty and continues in it, and is not a forgetful hearer but a doer of the work, this one will be blessed in what he does.

JAMES 1:22-25

PONDER THIS There is an important question we all must ask ourselves: What then shall I do with Jesus, who is called Christ? This question is personal. You, like Pilate, must answer it. This is a pertinent question. We're not talking about some personality. We're not talking about some denomination. We're not talking about some idea. We're talking about one who claims to be the Son of God. This question is pressing. It is before you right now. Everybody will answer one way or another, whether vocally or by their actions; they will answer this question.

Jesus Christ was in Pilate's hands that day. And today Jesus Christ is in your hand. But the time came when Pilate was in Jesus' hand, and the time will come when you will be in Jesus' hand. Jesus was standing before Pilate, but at the judgment, Pilate stood before Jesus. Jesus is standing before you today, through the Spirit and through the Word. But one day, you will stand before the Lord Jesus Christ. So, what will you do with Jesus, who is called Christ?

- How have you answered this important question? How has your answer impacted your life?

- Is this question foundational in your life? Why or why not? What needs to change?

PRACTICE THIS Talk to a minister or missionary who has dedicated his or her life to the cause of Christ and ask for insight on how this question has changed that person's life.

PRAY OVER THIS

Because what may be known of God is manifest in them,
for God has shown *it* to them. For since the creation of
the world His invisible attributes are clearly seen, being
understood by the things that are made, even His eternal
power and Godhead, so that they are without excuse.

ROMANS 1:19-20

PONDER THIS If you have a creation, you have to have a Creator. Today's text says the Creator is "clearly seen...by the things that are made." When I see a piano that's finely tuned, I know somebody crafted it. When I see a watch that runs with precision, I know somebody crafted that watch. When I see a building put together in symmetry and balance and purpose, I know there is an architect. And when I see this mighty Universe put together, when I see creation, I say, "There must be a Creator." When I see order and system, I say, "Intelligence." That's the reason the Bible says, "The fool has said in his heart, 'There's no God'" (Psalm 14:1a).

There is also the inward witness, the conscience. All people on the face of the Earth have these two witnesses: One is the outward, objective witness called creation; the other is the inward, subjective witness called conscience. This is a built-in knowledge of God. God made man to serve Him and to know Him. Until we do, we're like a round peg in a square hole, out of fellowship.

- How have you seen evidence of God in creation?

- Why is it important to remember we are made to serve God?

PRACTICE THIS Take a walk in nature and praise God for the outward and inward witness to Him.

66

PRAY OVER THIS

For I am not ashamed of the gospel of Christ, for it
is the power of God to salvation for everyone who
believes, for the Jew first and also for the Greek.

ROMANS 1:16

PONDER THIS All men have some light, but light refused increases darkness. The thing about light is that it is not tangible, something you can hold. You cannot take light or truth and put it on ice. You cannot put truth in your pocket and say, "That's very interesting, I'll spend it someday if I need it." No, when God gives us light, when creation and conscience speak to the heart of any individual, if we do not glorify God, believe in God, and trust God, then we do not remain static. Instead, we begin to regress, and we lose even the light we have. Our foolish hearts will be darkened. We refuse truth because of the sin that is in our hearts.

Why do we not believe in God? Because belief in God means we must adjust our lifestyle. Our lifestyle, on one hand, is our unrighteousness, but on the other hand, there is creation and conscience. And so, creation and conscience tell us there's a God. Our lifestyle says, "If I admit that, I'm going to have to change this." So, we're in disagreement between the two. This is the struggle that goes back and forth. We may get the lifestyle we want, but it is a terrible trade-off to miss a relationship with the living God!

- Do you know people who are wrestling with their faith? What questions are they wrestling with? How might you support them?

- What are the things that had to change in your life when you started following Jesus?

PRACTICE THIS Pray for people who are wrestling with the decision to follow Jesus today.

PRAY OVER THIS

These things I have written to you who believe in the name of the Son of God, that you may know that you have eternal life, and that you may continue to believe in the name of the Son of God.

1 JOHN 5:13

PONDER THIS At Christmastime, you may go to buy a Christmas tree. You say, "Let's get a live tree this year." So, you go and buy a tree that's been cut. By New Year's, it is evident that this is no longer a live tree; we just call it that. It looks alive, but it has been cut off from the source of life. The reality will show up around New Year's. A lot of people decorate themselves and come to church on Sunday morning, but they're spiritually dead. Their mind, emotions, and will are operating. Their bodies are operating, but minus God in the spirit.

What do we have to do to be lost? Rob a bank? No! Commit murder? No! Take part in a scandal? No! To be lost requires nothing because we are lost by nature. We are born with a depraved nature. The Bible teaches that we are "by nature the children of wrath" who inherited that nature from Adam. (See Ephesians 2:3.) You can be so-called fine, upstanding, wonderful, and religious. God told Nicodemus—a better man outwardly, morally, and religiously than most—that he had to be born again to see the kingdom of God. (See John 3:3.) So, what does it mean to be lost? It simply means to be without God.

- What evidence does your life give of your relationship with God?

- What are some ways we "decorate" ourselves to fit in at church?

PRACTICE THIS Read John 15 with a friend and discuss what it looks like to be connected to God's life.

PRAY OVER THIS

I have manifested Your name to the men whom You have given Me out of the world. They were Yours, You gave them to Me, and they have kept Your word. Now they have known that all things which You have given Me are from You. For I have given to them the words which You have given Me; and they have received them, and have known surely that I came forth from You; and they have believed that You sent Me.

JOHN 17:6-8

PONDER THIS The reason some of us don't understand the Bible any more than we do is that we have not been living up to the light God has already given us. Why should God show you more in the Word of God until you obey what you already know? Isn't that a good question? You have excuses about why you don't obey basic calls of Scripture, then you're reading a passage of Scripture and thinking, "I wonder why I don't understand this. God show me what this means." God says, "Why should I show you what that means? You haven't obeyed what I've already shown you." If you want to understand the part of the Bible you don't understand, begin to obey the part you do understand. God will give you more as you're faithful with what you've received.

The problem is not in the head; the problem is in the heart. When a person surrenders his or her will, God will speak. Light obeyed increases light! Live up to the light that you have, and God will give you more.

- What are some commands in Scripture you struggle to follow?

- What does it look like to surrender your will to God?

PRACTICE THIS Talk to a mentor in the faith about the areas of Scripture you have struggled to follow.

PRAY OVER THIS

And this is the condemnation, that the light has come into the
world, and men loved darkness rather than light, because their
deeds were evil. For everyone practicing evil hates the light and
does not come to the light, lest his deeds should be exposed.
But he who does the truth comes to the light, that his deeds
may be clearly seen, that they have been done in God.

JOHN 3:19-21

PONDER THIS I was speaking to a young man who was struggling with doubt, and I asked him if he was an honest doubter or a dishonest doubter. I explained, "An honest doubter doesn't know, but he wants to know, and therefore he investigates. A dishonest doubter doesn't know because he doesn't want to know, and he can't find God for the same reason a thief can't find a policeman." Jesus said, "They hate the light, and they will not come to the light because their deeds are evil."

Would you like to find out whether you're an honest doubter or a dishonest doubter? Would you sign this statement: God, I don't know whether You exist or not. I don't know whether the Bible is Your Word or not. I don't know whether Jesus Christ is Your Son or not. I don't know, but I want to know. And because I want to know, I will make an honest investigation. And because it is an honest investigation, I will follow the results of that investigation wherever they lead me, regardless of the cost. Would you sign that statement? We have to start with honesty with God, but it will require something of us. The decision to follow Jesus will require that we surrender our lives to Him when we recognize He is the way, the truth, and the life. (See John 14:6.)

- When have you struggled with doubt? Based on the assessment above, did you come to God honestly? Why or why not?

- What are some doubts you're struggling with right now? What have you done about them?

PRACTICE THIS Write down some of your doubts on a piece of paper, then go through each one, submitting it to God.

PRAY OVER THIS

For when we were still without strength, in due time Christ
died for the ungodly. For scarcely for a righteous man will
one die; yet perhaps for a good man someone would even
dare to die. But God demonstrates His own love toward us,
in that while we were still sinners, Christ died for us.

ROMANS 5:6-8

PONDER THIS Let me give you the best definition of sin I know: sin is coming
short of the glory of God. (See Romans 3:23.) Sin is everything in us that's not like
God. There's a lot of it, isn't there? We have all sinned and come short of the glory
of God. Don't stretch yourself out in the gutter alongside some clear hypocrite
and say, "I'm better than he is." So what? I hear people say, "Well, I'm just as good
as those people down there at the church." I'm looking for a man who's honest
enough to say, "I'm just as bad as those people down there at the church."
All have sinned and come short of the glory of God. That means me; that means
you; that means us; and that means every mother's child. God is in Heaven and
man is on Earth, and between them is the great chasm of sin that separates.
Repeatedly, man has tried to reach God, but he can't overcome the sin barrier on
his own power or goodness.

If sin is our part, what has God done? God came down to Earth. He, in glory, stepped
out of Heaven. God looked down at us and knew we could never overcome
that barrier on our own. God loved us while we were sinners, and He made the
permanent solution to the problem we could never take care of on our own.

- Why do you think we tend to compare ourselves to others?
  What is the danger in that?

- When have you tried to handle your sin in your own power?
  What happened?

PRACTICE THIS Pray for someone you know who needs the hope of the Gospel
in his or her life.

71

PRAY OVER THIS

You have neither part nor portion in this matter, for your heart is not right in the sight of God. Repent therefore of this your wickedness, and pray God if perhaps the thought of your heart may be forgiven you. For I see that you are poisoned by bitterness and bound by iniquity. Then Simon answered and said, "Pray to the Lord for me, that none of the things which you have spoken may come upon me."

ACTS 8:21-24

PONDER THIS There are so many who say, "I'm a believer," but they are not saved. You know the plan, but you don't know the Man. You've seen what God has done, but there has never been a change of heart. You say, "Well, doesn't the Bible say, 'Believe on the Lord Jesus Christ, and you will be saved?" (See Acts 16:31.) Yes, it does. The Bible also says, "Even the demons believe—and tremble!" (James 2:19c). There's a superficial faith of false religion; the kind of faith that never really comes and bows the knee to Jesus Christ, never makes Jesus Christ Lord.

John 2:23-24 says, "Now when He was in Jerusalem at the Passover, during the feast, many believed in His name when they saw the signs which He did. But Jesus did not commit Himself to them, because He knew all men." Now you don't see it in English, but in Greek, the word for believe and commit is the same word, just translated differently. So, you could say, "Many committed themselves to Him, but He did not commit Himself to them." Or "Many believed in Him, but He did not believe in them." They believed in Him like Simon the sorcerer, but He did not believe in them.

The Lord knows your heart. You may have walked the aisle and prayed the prayer, but He knows what is superficial. Has your faith shaped how you have lived since your moment of confession, or have you been faking it with all the right language and answers?

- What is the difference between knowing the plan of salvation and knowing the Man of salvation, Jesus?

- How has your faith shaped how you have lived? What has stayed the same?

PRACTICE THIS Talk to a pastor about what it means to live out a sincere and true faith.

72

PRAY OVER THIS

All Scripture is given by inspiration of God, and is profitable
for doctrine, for reproof, for correction, for instruction in
righteousness, that the man of God may be complete,
thoroughly equipped for every good work.

2 TIMOTHY 3:16-17

PONDER THIS The Bible is like a garment: You can pull a thread here, and it wrinkles way down at the bottom. The Bible is one book, but it is composed of sixty-six books. There are thirty-nine books in the Old Testament and twenty-seven books in the New Testament. At least forty different authors wrote these books over about sixteen hundred years. They were written in about thirteen different countries and on three different continents. People from all kinds of backgrounds wrote them: some were shepherds; some were kings; some were soldiers; some were princes; some were priests; some were fishermen; some were scholars; some were historians; some were business and professional men; and others were common laborers. They wrote on many different subjects, and they wrote from different backgrounds, in at least three different languages. Yet when these books come together, they don't make sixty-six separate books. From Genesis to Revelation, the Bible reads as one book. There is an incredible unity in the Bible.

All the Bible is kind of summed up in this: "Jesus loves me, this I know. For the Bible tells me so!" God loves you. This Book tells us that Jesus left Heaven, came, suffered, bled, and died for your sin. God raised Him from the dead. He ascended to Heaven, and if you will trust Him and surrender your life to Him, He will save you and keep you according to the Word of God.

- When have you been convinced of the truth in God's Word? When have you struggled to trust it?

- Why is it important to recognize the unity in God's Word?

PRACTICE THIS Praise God for the unity and intentionality in His Word.

73

PRAY OVER THIS

"And when you pray, you shall not be like the hypocrites. For they love to pray standing in the synagogues and on the corners of the streets, that they may be seen by men...But you, when you pray, go into your room, and when you have shut your door, pray to your Father who is in the secret place; and your Father who sees in secret will reward you openly. And when you pray, do not use vain repetitions...For your Father knows the things you have need of before you ask Him."

MATTHEW 6:5-8

PONDER THIS Jesus is not opposed to public prayer. What He is opposed to is praying to be seen by men. This reminds me of a young lawyer who had just gone into business. He hung out his sign in front of his brand-new law office. He didn't have one client. When he heard someone walking down the hallway, he thought, "Perhaps this is a client I can impress." So, he picked up the phone, and nobody was on the other end of the line. He made up a story and said, "No, I'm sorry. I've got a heavy corporation case. I may be able to help you, but I'm very busy. Good-bye." By that time, the man who walked down the hall had arrived in his office and said, "I'm from the telephone company. I came to hook up your telephone." That's the kind of prayer that our Lord is talking about—when there's nobody on the other end of the line. We're simply praying to be seen and heard by others.

Why do we pray? We do not pray to impress people, but we also don't pray to impress God. It's not the logic of our prayer, and it's not the language of our prayer that impresses God. You don't have to be a minister or poet to pray. It is really quite simple. Can you talk? Can you talk to another human being? Can you not talk to God? You don't have to spin your wheels to impress Him or other people. Just come and talk to Him.

- What is something important happening in your life that you need to talk to God about?

- What does your prayer life look like? What are the occasions that you pray? What are the different things you pray for?

PRACTICE THIS Take a prayer walk and talk to God as you move through your neighborhood.

74

PRAY OVER THIS

And we are witnesses of all things which He did both in the land of the Jews and in Jerusalem, whom they killed by hanging on a tree. Him God raised up on the third day, and showed Him openly, not to all the people, but to witnesses chosen before by God, even to us who ate and drank with Him after He arose from the dead. And He commanded us to preach to the people, and to testify that it is He who was ordained by God to be Judge of the living and the dead.

ACTS 10:39-42

PONDER THIS There must be personal confidence when you start to share your faith. If you're not sure about your own faith, you're not going to make a soul winner. Peter said, "We are witnesses of all things which He did." That is a powerful statement! There is no reasonable way on earth to dispute the witness of these early apostles. You think about who was witnessing. These twelve apostles gave a united witness of what they'd seen and heard, saying, "We are eyewitnesses."

They were a very different group of people with the same conclusion. Think about the category of persons. There was the Apostle John, who was young, observant, and philosophical. There was Peter, a loudmouth fisherman. There was Simon, who was a political zealot. Nathaniel and Thomas were somewhat skeptical. Matthew was a little dishonest in his business before he got saved. Andrew was kind and compassionate.

In the Body of Christ, there are so many different kinds of people. What would happen if we went into a church and asked the question, "What holds you people together? How do you have this unity? Where does this spirit come from? What is the glue that holds the Church together?" Is it preferences? Is it race? Is it culture? No, it has been and always should be Jesus. We're so different, but we need to come together in unity around the One we know and worship.

- Do you experience unity with the Body of Christ? Why or why not?

- What gives you confidence in your faith? How do you share that with others?

PRACTICE THIS Talk to a friend from church about what it looks like to have only Christ in common.

76

(75)

For whatever things were written before were written
for our learning, that we through the patience and
comfort of the Scriptures might have hope.

ROMANS 15:4

PONDER THIS The Bible has one theme: salvation. The Bible has one hero, Jesus. It has one villain: the devil. There is one purpose: to glorify God. How do you explain the unity of the Bible apart from divine inspiration? That's the reason we believe the Bible is the Word of God.

It is not only unified in message but also in events. The prophecies in Scripture and how accurately they are fulfilled are evidence of the truth of the Bible. When you read the prophecies of the Bible, you have to stand back in awe. The subject of prophecy is so big that I could not even begin to deal with it. It would be like trying to dip out an entire ocean with a teacup. So, let's just talk about the prophecies concerning the central character of the Bible: the Lord Jesus. There are more than three hundred precise prophecies that deal with the Lord Jesus Christ in the Old Testament that are fulfilled by Jesus in the New Testament. To say these are fulfilled by chance is an astronomical impossibility. Jesus infinitely fulfilled prophecy. The Bible is more than a book. Jesus is more than a man. Wherever you are in life, this Word of Life applies to you. Whatever situation you find yourself in, Jesus is the hope you need.

- What fulfilled biblical prophecies can you name?

- How have you seen unity in Scripture? How does this build your faith?

PRACTICE THIS Read the Bible with a friend and discuss how it has impacted your life.

PRAY OVER THIS

The word which God sent to the children of Israel, preaching
peace through Jesus Christ—He is Lord of all—that word
you know, which was proclaimed throughout all Judea, and
began from Galilee after the baptism which John preached:
how God anointed Jesus of Nazareth with the Holy Spirit
and with power, who went about doing good and healing all
who were oppressed by the devil, for God was with Him.

ACTS 10:36-38

PONDER THIS I was in Moscow over Easter on a trip for a preaching engagement. After the event, we decided to visit the tomb of Lenin, the leader of the Soviet people. It was such an experience to see the crystal sarcophagus. They had embalmed his body and kept it in wonderful condition. There, inscribed in the tomb, it read: "He was the greatest leader of all peoples, of all countries, of all times. He was the lord of all humanity. He was the savior of the world." One thing to notice: it's all past tense. He was the lord. He was the savior. He was the greatest. What a contrast from our faith. Jesus is the greatest. Jesus is the Lord. He is the Savior.

When Peter gave witness to Jesus, he essentially said, "We saw it. We saw His virtuous life. We saw His vicarious death. We saw His victorious resurrection. And this is what we want to share with you." Peter was totally convinced. Are you totally convinced? Not only are we witnesses; we ought to be part of the evidence. Jesus as Lord should be evident in how we live and submit to Him. Jesus is alive and should be evident in our hope, even when all seems like it has gone wrong.

- Why is it important to remember Jesus as our living and continuing hope?

- When have you been hurt or felt like all hope was gone? How has hope in Jesus helped you through these moments?

PRACTICE THIS Discuss with another believer how Jesus being our living Lord changes life today.

PRAY OVER THIS

The statutes of the LORD are right, rejoicing the heart;
the commandment of the LORD is pure, enlightening the
eyes; the fear of the LORD is clean, enduring forever; The
judgments of the LORD are true and righteous altogether.

PSALM 19:8-9

PONDER THIS Do you want to be a true intellectual? Get in the Word of God—it is sure. What does that mean? It means you've got a firm place to stand. You have a foundation. You're not building on Jell-O. Any ordinary person can go to God's Word and receive food for the soul. Verse 8a says, "The statutes of the Lord are right, rejoicing the heart." The word *right* here has the idea of a straight path. The Bible will never lead you astray. Hallelujah for that! You know, so many times we think God's will is hard and God's way is burdensome. But this verse says, "The statutes of the Lord are right, rejoicing the heart." Oh, how we should delight in the Word of God. What a joy there is in knowing God's Word. His way is the way of joy. If I had a thousand lives, I would give them all to the Lord Jesus Christ.

There are no seeds of corruption in God's Word. It will last forever. It's been several millennia since David wrote this psalm, and we're holding it in our hands today. "The grass withers, the flower fades, but the word of our God stands forever" (Isaiah 40:8). The Bible is never out of date. It applies to every age, and it is relevant to your life today.

- What are some ways you would describe God's Word?

- Who in your life takes joy in God's Word? How is that evident?

PRACTICE THIS Talk to a mentor in the faith and ask that person for the secret to growing in the Lord.

PRAY OVER THIS

For unto us a Child is born, unto us a Son is given;
and the government will be upon His shoulder. And
His name will be called Wonderful, Counselor, Mighty
God, Everlasting Father, Prince of Peace.

ISAIAH 9:6

PONDER THIS The baby Jesus was born King. We didn't elect Him, and we'll not impeach Him. He is King. He is Lord. Some ask, "Have you made Him Lord?" But you're too late for that. God has already declared Him Lord. This is His sovereign nobility and right. He is King of kings and Lord of lords. The question is not whether He is Lord, but whether you have recognized His place in your life. He is Lord, but do you live like it? Do you stand in awe of Him? If not, the problem is not with Him but with us. Jesus is incomprehensibly wonderful.

A man was riding on a train, looking out the window and saying, "Wonderful, wonderful, wonderful." The man sitting next to him asked, "Why do you think everything is wonderful?" He said, "I've been blind. I've just had surgery, and I'm seeing things that I had long since forgotten how beautiful they were. They are wonderful to me." If Jesus is not wonderful to you, you need your spiritual eyes opened to see just how wonderful Jesus is.

- How have you recognized Jesus' position as Lord over your life? What areas are difficult to surrender to Him?

- How has your awe of Jesus changed over time? Is this positive or negative? Why?

PRACTICE THIS Take time to marvel at God whether through prayer, song, or journaling.

PRAY OVER THIS

He spoke of Judas Iscariot, the son of Simon, for it was
he who would betray Him, being one of the twelve.

JOHN 6:71

PONDER THIS Judas had the right stuff. If you had looked at Judas, you would've said, "What a great guy this man Judas is." He had the right associations. He was close with Jesus. Jesus called him a friend. He spent three and a half years in the best seminary in the world, studying with the Lord Jesus Christ, learning, and hearing Jesus teach.

Not only did he have the right associations, but he also had the right reputation. When Jesus was at the last supper and said, "One of you will betray Me" (John 13:21c), the others didn't say, "Oh, I know, it must be Judas." Do you know what job Judas had? Judas was the treasurer. He was the man who had the money bag. Who do you make treasurer? The person who has the most integrity; the person you respect the most. He was a worker. He went out with the others when they went out to teach, to preach, and to do good. He was right in it with the group.

We have people like that in church all the time. You're a Bible-believing person; you've got good associations. You've got a good reputation: everybody thinks you're a wonderful person, and you may be outwardly. You do a lot of good things: you may be singing in the choir, taking the offering, teaching a Sunday school class, or doing something wonderful. But your heart is far from God. The external things mean nothing if you are just going through the motions.

- If you are honest with yourself, what is your relationship like with God right now? Are you devoted to Him, or is your heart far from Him?

- Why are we easily tempted to do external things to impress others instead of actually being right with God?

PRACTICE THIS Pray for your fellow Christians, asking God to keep their hearts devoted to Him.

PRAY OVER THIS

For Christ also suffered once for sins, the just for the unjust, that He might bring us to God, being put to death in the flesh but made alive by the Spirit.

1 PETER 3:18

PONDER THIS God forgives sin, but how? There must be somebody who pays the penalty for sin. God cannot just overlook sin. If God were to overlook sin, God would no longer be holy any more than a judge would be a righteous judge if He were to overlook a crime.

There's a saying that goes, "When a guilty man is acquitted, the judge is condemned." If a judge were to just say, "I'm a loving judge. I will overlook rape, murder, arson, robbery, whatever it is. That's all right. I'm a loving judge." At that moment, the judge becomes a criminal.

If God were to simply overlook sin without punishing it, God would topple from His throne of holiness. If there'd been some other way for you to have been saved, God would have taken it. That's the reason the Apostle Paul said, "I am not ashamed of the gospel of Christ, for it is the power of God to salvation..." (Romans 1:16a). Jesus died for you, and He wants you to live a life that glorifies Him and shares that hope with others.

- How necessary is the cross?

- What level of urgency do you feel to share the message of the cross with others?

PRACTICE THIS Think of someone you know who needs the hope of Jesus and find a way to serve that person.

PRAY OVER THIS

Blessed be the God and Father of our Lord Jesus Christ, who has blessed us with every spiritual blessing in the heavenly places in Christ, just as He chose us in Him before the foundation of the world, that we should be holy and without blame before Him in love.

EPHESIANS 1:3-4

PONDER THIS The word *holy* means God is the opposite of sin. God is righteous and holy, and sin must be punished. God cannot overlook sin.

The world rejects the idea of sin. But God, who is infinite love, has a holy hatred for sin. So, God had in His heart a plan by which sin could be punished and man could be forgiven through substitution. Sometimes we have the idea that we can come to God because of our good works and best efforts, but all our attempts can do nothing before Him. We need the cross. Did you know the Bible says we are reconciled to God by the death of His Son? (See 2 Corinthians 5:18-21.) God is not reconciled to you. We're the sinners. We're the ones who need to be made right. And we have no way to come to God except through the cross.

- What are some ways you have tried to impress God?

- Why is it important to remember we are reconciled to God instead of the other way around?

PRACTICE THIS Write a thank-you note to God for the cross and for the reconciliation He provides.

PRAY OVER THIS

...who Himself bore our sins in His own body on
the tree, that we, having died to sins, might live for
righteousness—by whose stripes you were healed.

1 PETER 2:24

PONDER THIS I want you to imagine a scene: They took Jesus and nailed Him to the cross. There were two thieves, one on each side. But those crosses were put up for three thieves: the two thieves who were crucified, and Barabbas. It was Barabbas's cross. Imagine the soldier, with a torch, goes down a narrow corridor in a dingy Roman jail. He comes to a certain cell. The guard stops and says, "You are free to go. Barabbas, you're not going to die. Do you see those three crosses? See the middle cross? That cross was made for you. But Pilate says you're going to go free. That man up there is dying in your place." I don't know what came of Barabbas, but isn't it wonderful how God arranges the whole thing so we can learn and see the lesson of substitution?

You say, "Christ died for me." That's true, but may I ask you to tweak it just a little bit? Instead, say this to yourself today: "Christ died instead of me." That's what it is. The purpose of the cross is one of substitution. Barabbas was a thief; we're thieves. We are supposed to have been God's stewards, and we failed. Barabbas was a rebel. We're meant to be God's servants, and we've rejected Him. Barabbas was a murderer, and we are responsible for the death of God's Son. Barabbas was a prisoner, and we have been bound with sin. He represents us all.

- How easily do you recognize your sin as deserving of death? Why does this matter?

- Why is understanding that Christ died "instead of me" important in our faith?

PRACTICE THIS Write down the statement "Christ died instead of me" and put it up somewhere you will be regularly reminded of this truth.

PRAY OVER THIS

For He made Him who knew no sin to be sin for us, that
we might become the righteousness of God in Him.

2 CORINTHIANS 5:21

PONDER THIS There was a cup Jesus drank from. What was in that cup? Imagine if you put all of your sin in a cup, then passed that cup to the billions of people who are alive on the face of the Earth and let them put their sin in. Then, you go back through time from Adam and Eve up until the day the trumpet shall sound and time shall be no more, and let every person put their sin in that cup. That is the cup Jesus took. He took that filthy cup, and He drank it down. He did not become a sinner, but He became sin.

When I read about Gethsemane, I want to weep. The very Son of God, with black dirt and red blood on His face, was praying, "Father, if it is possible, let this cup pass from Me" (Matthew 26:39b). Jesus knew when He took that cup, when He took the full weight of sin on Himself, God would have to treat Jesus as God treats sin, because Jesus was the substitute. God "did not spare His own Son" (Romans 8:32a). Jesus knew that He, who had been in the bosom of the Father from all eternity, would become the object of the Father's wrath. He would be separated from God the Father. This is what took place so you and I could have unity with our heavenly Father. What a beautiful and costly gift.

- How do you feel when you consider all Jesus went through so you could be reconciled to God?

- Do you treat unity with God as something valuable? Why or why not?

PRACTICE THIS Pray for someone you know who has not received this precious gift from God.

PRAY OVER THIS

Pilate said to them, "What then shall I do with Jesus who is called Christ?" They all said to him, "Let Him be crucified!"

MATTHEW 27:22

PONDER THIS In Matthew 27, Jesus stood on trial before Pilate. In this account, we come face-to-face with the most present, pressing, and pertinent question ever asked: Is Jesus God as He claimed to be? If He is not, then He is a fraud, an imposter, and a deceiver. What we decide about Jesus will dictate eternity for each of us. Scripture gives us so much evidence that Jesus is God.

First, the attributes of God the Father are found in Jesus.

Throughout the Gospels, we find that Jesus was the fulfillment of the prophecies of the Old Testament. He is described as God is described in Psalms and Isaiah: the King of Glory, the first and the last, the Lord of Hosts.

He is also shown to be God by the adoration He received.

Jesus also said He is God. In John 8:58, Jesus said, "Most assuredly, I say to you, before Abraham was, I AM." By quoting Exodus 3:14, Jesus claimed to be God.

Each of us has the opportunity, like Pilate, to decide what we do with Jesus. We can either accept Him or reject Him, love or despise Him, but we cannot be neutral. What do you believe about Jesus Christ: Will you crown Him or crucify Him? I love Him with all my heart. To explain Him is impossible; to ignore Him is disastrous; and to reject Him is fatal.

- What have you decided to do with the claims of Jesus?

- What difference does this decision make to your daily life?

PRACTICE THIS Consider the areas of your life you have not given to God. Pray and surrender those things to Him today.

PRAY OVER THIS

And He was withdrawn from them about a stone's throw, and He
knelt down and prayed, saying, "Father, if it is Your will, take this
cup away from Me; nevertheless not My will, but Yours, be done."
Then an angel appeared to Him from heaven, strengthening Him.

LUKE 22:41-43

PONDER THIS Jesus paid a price. You will never know the agony the Son of God endured on the cross. He didn't have to die; He had a choice. And Jesus said, "Nevertheless not My will, but Yours, be done." Adam, following Satan in the garden of Eden, said, "Not thy will, but mine," and ruined the race. Jesus, in another garden, as the last Adam said, "not My will, but Yours," and redeemed the race. That's the consumption of the cup. The Lord Jesus willingly, voluntarily, vicariously, and victoriously said, "...not My will, but Yours" (Luke 22:42b). Had He said no, every one of us would have been separated from God forever. But because Jesus suffered, bled, and died on that cross, you and I can be redeemed. Jesus took my sin and your sin, and He carried it to the cross.

In today's passage, Jesus was wrestling. Was He wrestling with God the Father? No, never. The great desire of his heart was to please the Father. Was He wrestling with Satan? He never needed to. He had absolute authority over Satan. He was wrestling with Himself. He was wrestling between His humanity and His love, but where did He land? "Not My will, but Yours, be done."

- When was a time you fought to get your way with God? How did that turn out?

- How would your life look different if you chose to say, "not my will, but Yours, be done"?

PRACTICE THIS Consider one area of your life where you are holding onto your own will and way over God's. Ask Him for direction and help.

PRAY OVER THIS

When they had twisted a crown of thorns, they put it on His head,
and a reed in His right hand. And they bowed the knee before
Him and mocked Him, saying, "Hail, King of the Jews!" Then they
spat on Him, and took the reed and struck Him on the head.
And when they had mocked Him, they took the robe off Him,
put His own clothes on Him, and led Him away to be crucified.

MATTHEW 27:29-31

PONDER THIS Some years ago in New York City, there was a mother who was hanging clothes to dry outside when a fire broke out in her home with her baby inside. That mother's face took the heat of those flames and was horribly scarred. Her hands were burned, but the baby was not touched at all by that fire. Not a hair was singed. One day, that girl grew up and spoke to a friend who said, "Who is that hideous woman?" This girl said, "I don't know," and the mother heard.

Later, when they got home, the mother said, "Darling, come here. I want to tell you something. When you were a baby, I went into a burning house and rescued you; not a hair on your head was touched, but these scars on my face and these scars on my hand are there because I rescued you from the flames." When that daughter learned the truth, she was filled with shame and remorse. She said, "Oh, my mother, can you ever forgive me?" Let us never be ashamed of Jesus and the scars He bore for our sake. How could we ever blush to speak His name or own His cause? Jesus wore my crown. The sacred mystery is that He bore the curse; the solemn misery is that He suffered our hell.

- What does it look like to live ashamed of Jesus? To live unashamed?
- Where is it difficult for you to live unashamed for Jesus?

PRACTICE THIS Discuss with a close Christian friend what it means to live unashamed of Jesus.

87

PRAY OVER THIS

And if you call on the Father, who without partiality judges according
to each one's work, conduct yourselves throughout the time of
your stay here in fear; knowing that you were not redeemed with
corruptible things, like silver or gold, from your aimless conduct
received by tradition from your fathers, but with the precious
blood of Christ, as of a lamb without blemish and without spot.

1 PETER 1:17-19

PONDER THIS In Exodus 12, God instituted the ritual of the Passover lamb. There was judgment on the land because of sin, but God told His people to take a spotless lamb, without blemish, and kill it. The blood was to be shed at each household, and they were to put the blood on the doorpost of each house—not on the inside, but on the outside. They were to be openly, publicly unashamed of the blood of the lamb. What had they done? They had made the sign of the cross. Even there, so long ago, God pictured the sacrifice of His Son. And God said, "When I see the blood, I will pass over you" (Exodus 12:13b). And that is where we get the name, Passover. God will pass over you when the blood is applied. If you put the blood beneath your feet and pass over the blood, God will not pass over you. But when you put yourself under the blood, the judgment of Almighty God will pass over you. And this Passover lamb was a picture of the ultimate Lamb of God, the Lord Jesus Christ.

- How does it encourage you to know Jesus fulfills the prophecy of the Old Testament?

- How often do you reflect on the reality that God has passed over your sin because of Jesus, our Passover Lamb?

PRACTICE THIS Write down some of the things you have been carrying guilt or shame about and submit those things to God.

88

PRAY OVER THIS

Now when they saw the boldness of Peter and John, and
perceived that they were uneducated and untrained men, they
marveled. And they realized that they had been with Jesus.

ACTS 4:13

PONDER THIS How did these fishermen stand up and preach and see five thousand come to Christ? It was because He lives, and they were not dependent on their power of speech, their logic, or their winsomeness to bring these people to Christ. There was the living Christ inside of them. Anything I can talk you into, somebody else can talk you out of. We are not preaching facts about a dead Christ of history. We present the living Christ to you. Do you know what convinced Thomas? He had an encounter with the living Lord. (See John 20:24-29.) When he had an encounter with the living Christ, he was convinced. Do you know what you need today? An encounter with Jesus Christ. In Acts 4, these people were brought in contact, by the Holy Spirit, with the living Christ, and they were convinced.

You see, other leaders come and go. But Christ is risen. It is an encounter with the living Christ that convinces people. I don't have to depend on my ability to cause anyone to believe when I preach. My ability, my job, my joy, my responsibility is to bring you to an encounter with Jesus Christ. When you meet Christ, you will never be the same.

- Who in your life needs the hope of the living Christ?

- How is Christ different from every other leader people admire?

PRACTICE THIS Praise and thank God for the living hope you have in Jesus.

PRAY OVER THIS

For Christ also suffered once for sins, the just for the unjust, that He might bring us to God, being put to death in the flesh but made alive by the Spirit.

1 PETER 3:18

PONDER THIS There's a word I don't want you to miss in this passage: *once*. That does not mean once upon a time: it means once for all. When Jesus said, "It is finished!", He meant the debt had been paid for sin—absolutely and completely. (See John 19:30.) In Rome, when a man would be put in prison, they would write out a certificate of debt. This was his debt to society for his crime, and the document would be placed on his prison door. After he had done his time and paid the penalty, they would write across that certificate of debt.

Do you know the word they would write? *Tetalesti*. Do you know what that means? It is finished; it is paid in full. That man won't have to go back to prison again. If they arrest him for that crime again, he can say, "Yes, but I have paid. It is done. You can't bring me in twice for the same crime." Jesus has once suffered for sin. That means you cannot pay for it yourself through your good works or by beating yourself up with shame. It has already been done. Your debt is paid, and you are free to go and live for God.

- How have you tried to earn God's favor through good works? Why won't this ever work?

- How does the fact that your sin has been paid in full change your daily life?

PRACTICE THIS Be an encourager. Remind a fellow Christian today that his or her sin has been paid in full.

PRAY OVER THIS

For when we were still without strength, in
due time Christ died for the ungodly.

ROMANS 5:6

PONDER THIS Many of us do not realize we are spiritually paralyzed. You may think, *I'm not weak: I lift weights; I'm very strong*. I'm not talking about physical weakness. You may think, *I'm not weak: I have a PhD*. I'm not talking about intellectual weakness. You may think, *I'm not weak: I have a million dollars in the bank*. I'm not talking about financial weakness. I'm talking about spiritual weakness that has paralyzed you.

Our weakness is that we don't have the strength to be godly. God's plan for all of us is that we be godly. But we don't have the strength. I don't care how hard you try: you don't have what it takes to be godly. You may be strong enough to do as you want, but you're not strong enough to do as you ought. While we were yet without strength, Christ died for the ungodly. The primary source of our weakness is sin; the paralyzing force of our sin is that we cannot be what God would have us to be. But Christ has died for us in our greatest weakness.

- What are some weaknesses you often feel? Why do you think we often forget about our spiritual weakness?

- How can you seek to be godly in God's strength?

PRACTICE THIS Pray for someone you know who needs to work in God's strength.

Adrian **Rogers**, one of America's most respected Bible teachers, faithfully preached the Word of God for 53 years—32 of those years as senior pastor of the historic Bellevue Baptist Church near Memphis, Tennessee.

He wrote 18 books and over 80 booklets giving strength and encouragement on subjects such as marriage, prophecy, evangelism, and the Christian walk.

In 1987 he founded Love Worth Finding Ministries to communicate the glorious Gospel of Jesus Christ with millions around the world. The message of God's love continues today, and as he so aptly put it, "Truly, the sun never sets on the ministry of Love Worth Finding."

IF THIS DEVOTIONAL HAS BEEN A HELP TO YOU, WOULD YOU CONSIDER SOMETHING?

This ministry is made possible because of the generous support of people like you who believe in the mission of Love Worth Finding—to bring people to Christ and mature them in the faith.

Your gift today will help others hear the profound truth of the Gospel...simply stated by Pastor Adrian Rogers.

lwf.org/give

800-274-5683

LOVEWORTHFINDING®
WITH ADRIAN ROGERS

2941 Kate Bond Road | Memphis TN 38133 | (901) 382-7900